CW01509241

HUMANITARIAN LOGISTICS

INSEAD Business Press Series

J. Frank Brown
THE GLOBAL BUSINESS LEADER

David Fubini, Colin Price and Maurizio Zollo
MERGERS
Leadership, Performance and Corporate Health

Manfred Kets de Vries, Konstantin Korotov and Elizabeth
Florent-Treacy
COACH AND COUCH
The Psychology of Making Better Leaders

James Teboul
SERVICE IS FRONT STAGE
Positioning Services for Value Advantage

Jean-Claude Thoenig and Charles Waldman
THE MARKING ENTERPRISE
Business Success and Societal Embedding

Rolando Tomasini and Luk Van Wassenhove
HUMANITARIAN LOGISTICS

HUMANITARIAN LOGISTICS

Rolando Tomasini

and

Luk Van Wassenhove

© Rolando Tomasini and Luk Van Wassenhove 2009

All rights reserved. No reproduction, copy or transmission of this
publication may be made without written permission.

No portion of this publication may be reproduced, copied or transmitted
save with written permission or in accordance with the provisions of the
Copyright, Designs and Patents Act 1988, or under the terms of any licence
permitting limited copying issued by the Copyright Licensing Agency,
Saffron House, 6-10 Kirby Street, London EC1N 8TS.

Any person who does any unauthorized act in relation to this publication
may be liable to criminal prosecution and civil claims for damages.

The authors have asserted their rights to be identified
as the authors of this work in accordance with the Copyright,
Designs and Patents Act 1988.

First published 2009 by
PALGRAVE MACMILLAN

Palgrave Macmillan in the UK is an imprint of Macmillan Publishers Limited,
registered in England, company number 785998, of Houndmills, Basingstoke,
Hampshire RG21 6XS.

Palgrave Macmillan in the US is a division of St Martin's Press LLC,
175 Fifth Avenue, New York, NY 10010.

Palgrave Macmillan is the global academic imprint of the above companies
and has companies and representatives throughout the world.

Palgrave® and Macmillan® are registered trademarks in the United States,
the United Kingdom, Europe and other countries.

ISBN-13: 978–0–230–20575–8
ISBN-10: 0–230–20575–5

This book is printed on paper suitable for recycling and made from fully
managed and sustained forest sources. Logging, pulping and manufacturing
processes are expected to conform to the environmental regulations of the
country of origin.

A catalogue record for this book is available from the British Library.

A catalog record for this book is available from the Library of Congress.

10   9   8   7   6   5   4   3   2   1
18 17 16 15 14 13 12 11 10 09

Printed and bound in Great Britain by
CPI Antony Rowe, Chippenham and Eastbourne

To my siblings (Rolando)

CONTENTS

CONTENTS

CONTENTS

PROLOGUE

About seven years ago, we made a commitment to this topic, having very limited knowledge of the humanitarian world. Driven by the conviction that a lot could be learned from these exceptional types of operations, our group began to write case studies on humanitarian logistics with the UN agencies (Joint Logistics Centre and World Food Program), the International Federation of the Red Cross and Red Crescent, and FUNDESUMA.

Increasingly, we realized that the professionalization of logistics in the humanitarian sector was a pressing need toward which we could contribute. Motivated by the request of our humanitarian partners to partake in their trainings and activities, we continued to build our team at INSEAD, developing articles, case studies, and course packages.

As our knowledge of the area increased, so did the demand for more information, though this time from the private sector. This was when corporate social responsibility and public–private partnerships began to appear high on both sectors' agendas, raising questions about how and why should both sectors work together. We expanded our interests to include private–humanitarian relations, specifically how value could be created for both sectors through the exchange of best practices.

Overall, the process of getting to know the humanitarian sector has been a journey of discovering the different organizations (their structures, funding mechanisms, ideologies), the challenges they face responding to different types of unpredictable events around the world, and the complex environment in which donors, organizations, communities, and beneficiaries have to make decisions. Today we have a dedicated team of researchers, doctoral students, and faculty who have produced 30 case studies, 15 articles, several reports, an MBA elective, and an executive education program for humanitarian agencies. We are pleased that our work has received international recognition, in particular several awards. This book is heavily inspired by those publications.

This book presents an overview of this enriching experience. Chapters 1 and 2 define the link between logistics and humanitarianism, two areas that we connect through our research and work with the agencies and companies. Chapter 1 presents key concepts from supply chain management that we found most useful to understand and create parallels with the humanitarian world. Chapter 2 introduces key concepts from the humanitarian sector that define the parameters in which an emergency operation takes place.

Chapters 3 and 4 focus on the importance of working between (preparedness) and during (coordination) disasters to respond to the needs of the beneficiaries. Chapter 3 serves to explain the aspects of preparedness that need to be addressed to establish supply chain management as a core function in humanitarian organizations. Chapter 4 discusses the challenge of coordinating a response through the different stages of a disaster without command and control or a profit incentive.

Chapters 5 and 6 address two of the most crucial issues we encountered in our research: information and knowledge management. Chapter 5 discusses how to prioritize the flow of information to attain transparency and accountability, two very important factors to reduce politicization and manipulation of aid and improve planning. Chapter 6 explains how information can be turned into knowledge and integrated into organizations to improve their performance, an important element in light of high staff turnover and limited resources.

Chapter 7 returns to the departure point to analyze the areas in which supply chain management in the humanitarian sector can be improved. This time around we examine cross-learning opportunities between the humanitarian and the private sector through public–private partnerships and corporate social responsibility initiatives. The chapter explains how these partnerships are designed keeping in mind the cultural differences between the two sectors and the need to make partnerships sustainable.

We are most grateful to a large number of people and organizations for helping us bringing out this book. First, we would like to extend our gratitude to the humanitarian organizations with whom we have been involved: for the time and trust which they have invested in us; for sharing their experience with us through the numerous interviews, training sessions, field visits, and secondments; for their continuous support and engagement in our research. Most of them you will see portrayed in our cases, interviews, and examples.

We would also like to recognize INSEAD for all its support, the members of the Humanitarian Research Group and the Social Innovation Center, and our colleagues in academia for their advice and intellectual drive. We would especially like to thank Ramina Samii for her contribution to several of the case studies cited in this book and her dedication to our group. Similarly, we would like to thank our students for their feedback, dedication, and interest.

Finally, we would like to express our appreciation to our families and close friends for their support, encouragement, and understanding throughout this period of professional and personal dedication.

ROLANDO AND LUK

1

LOGISTICS OF HUMANITARIAN AID

INTRODUCTION

This chapter provides the reader with a brief introduction on logistics and supply chain management. It identifies the major supply chain issues in the humanitarian sector, particularly as they relate to emergencies and also reveals the need for cross-learning between the private and the humanitarian sector, a topic that we elaborate on throughout the book.

FROM LOGISTICS TO SUPPLY CHAIN MANAGEMENT

Getting different actors to work together by sharing processes and distribution channels requires a vision that goes beyond mere logistics. It requires an integrated supply chain management approach to effectively coordinate inter-agency performance, eliminate redundancies, and maximize efficiencies.

In the late 1980s and early 1990s, we saw an evolution from logistics as an activity (i.e., bringing products from point A to point B) to supply chain management as a necessary function in integrating complex global networks of design, procurement, manufacturing, distribution, and sale. This occurred in parallel with increased outsourcing of logistics activities to third-parties for reasons of cost as well as scope (*"logistics is not our core competence"*). Simultaneously, globalization trends pushed companies to look outside the box of their own company limits and pay attention to better coordination and integration of all activities along the total value chain. With globalization and increased outsourcing, the number of parties involved in bringing a simple product to a final consumer had significantly increased. Companies also started to recognize that all those parties contributed to the final consumer experience in terms of cost, quality, speed, variety, and innovation. The pieces of this now more complex puzzle needed to be coordinated. End-to-end supply chain management was born.[1]

Like the private sector, the humanitarians have had to look beyond basic logistics and use this supply chain management approach to coordinate the different players involved in a relief operation.

SUPPLY CHAIN MANAGEMENT

Using the supply chain management approach provides the opportunity to optimize logistical performance at the inter-organizational level. It also forces organizations to choose what capabilities along the value chain to invest in and develop internally, and which activities to allocate for development by suppliers.[2]

The use of supply chain management techniques is becoming more popular in the humanitarian arena, with cross-functional and inter-agency approaches becoming more common – at least in intent, if not execution. According to Handfield and Nichols,[3] the private sector experience shows that the emergence of supply chain management is also a result of the following factors.

The Information Revolution

Information today is cheaper, more accessible, more comprehensive and reliable, and easier to use for tracking the movement of materials. Databases are more powerful than ever. In the humanitarian world this is reflected by how quickly information about disasters becomes available, with on-site real-time broadcasting and reporting increasingly being the norm. This immediacy of information sets extraordinarily high expectations for rapid response and creates an even greater demand for advanced preparedness. Today, due to such global broadcasting networks like CNN, BBC, and Al-Jazeera, information reaches the general public often at the same time that it reaches specialized relief agencies.

Greater Pressure for *"Perfect Orders"*

As in the private sector, the public expects humanitarian supply chains to be more reactive (adaptable and agile) to the changing and sudden (and often unexpected) needs in the field. Because of the media spotlights (and immediacy of information), inefficiencies and mistakes in the supply chain are less tolerated.

New Forms of Inter-organizational Relationships

This increased pressure to execute "perfect orders," even in an emergency, has forced once insular and self-contained humanitarian agencies to break out of their silos and reach out to build new strategic relationships across sectors. Now more aware than ever of their own process shortcomings (through the application of relevant performance measures), and better able to identify process overlaps, gaps, and non–value-adding redundancies, the quality of inter-agency and cross-sector communication has improved.

These new forms of inter-organizational relationships are critical to effectively handle a growing demand for civil society to assist in emergencies. Greater information flow means people want to do something in reaction to the storm of media images now so common after a disaster. Many may want to volunteer or send aid in kind. Inter-agency coordination is critical in preventing the system from being clogged with their good, but sometimes mismanaged and uncoordinated intentions.

SUPPLY CHAIN MANAGEMENT FUNDAMENTALS: FLOWS, DESIGN, AND MANAGEMENT QUALITY

In the commercial sector, flows in supply chains are sometimes referred to as the Three Bs: Boxes, Bytes, and Bucks. In the humanitarian supply chain, we add a fourth and fifth B for Bodies and Brains, representing people, and their knowledge and skills.

Types of Flows in Supply Chains

- *Material* (*Boxes*): This represents the physical product flow from suppliers to customers as well as the reverse flow for product returns, servicing, and recycling.
- *Information* (*Bytes*): This represents the order transmission and order tracking which coordinates the physical flows.
- *Financial* (*Bucks*): This represents the credit terms, payment schedules, and consignment arrangements.

- *People* (*Bodies*): This represents all the manpower deployed at each intervention to implement the supply chain.
- *Knowledge and Skills* (*Brains*): This is particularly acute in the humanitarian sector since each time a supply chain is deployed in response to a disaster the required skills need to be quickly reconfigured; that is, every supply chain is new and different (see Figure 1.1).

All flows can be equally important and from a risk management perspective a disruption in one of them is likely to have a direct impact on the others. For example, a shortage of staff in customs clearance can stop relief goods from getting into a country. The lack of proper needs assessment can trigger a wave of unsolicited donations, or insufficient donations for the most urgent needs. The key is to combine

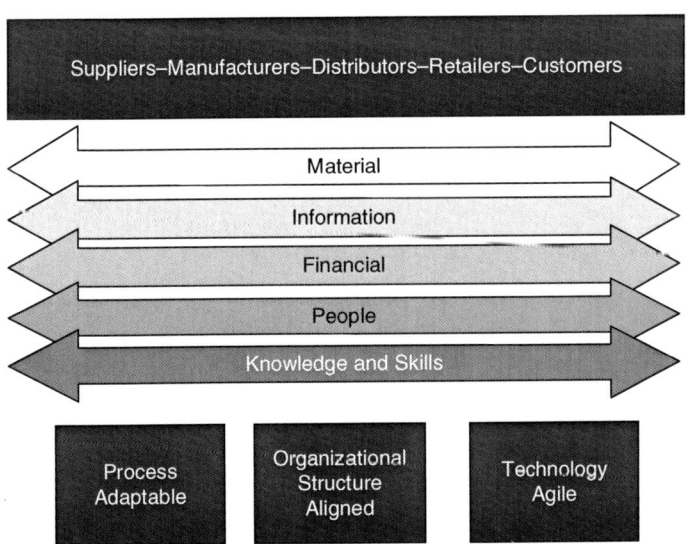

FIGURE 1.1 **The Supply Chain Flows**

all five flows into a flawless execution plan to produce an adequate response.

Supply Chain Design

The five Bs of disaster supply chain flows need to be supported by a coherent business model and an appropriate design of the system executing the flows from end to end. Whereas a coherent business model is hard enough to define for commercial businesses, it is extremely difficult for humanitarian organizations to figure out what exactly the goal is. Sure, one can formulate general objectives like saving lives or helping people in need, but how exactly does one measure the success of a humanitarian intervention? Businesses are driven by customers (demand), while humanitarian organizations are mostly driven by donors (supply). Beneficiaries (customers) have very little power. This lack of customer pressure makes it harder for humanitarian organizations to pursue their objectives (e.g., donors or beneficiaries?).

There are three basic design pillars to a supply chain (see Figure 1.1):

- *Processes and Product Structures*: The conceptual design of products and processes has a large impact on supply chain performance potential. For instance, modularity enables the response to be adaptable to the specific needs of the environment. Modularity can apply to value-added processes such as logistics, as well as to new products or services.
- *Organizational Structures*: Decisions on how the organization is structured – for example, who gets what information, who decides on what, and how are people evaluated

and rewarded – also have a huge impact on supply chain performance. If designed properly, organizational structures enable the response to be aligned among the different stakeholders. Organizational structures range from total vertical integration to networked companies, and encompass a range of relationships to develop the necessary trust over time. Performance management and reward schemes are critical in influencing the behavior of the system, and can act as the glue that keeps the whole value system together.

- *Technologies*: Technologies, in particular information and communications technologies, can be a powerful lubricant for supply chains. Appropriate information systems enable the response to be more agile, that is adjusting itself to dynamic changes in the environment as the disaster develops.

Throughout the book, we will discuss in greater detail the importance of having a supply chain that is adaptable, agile and aligned, that is a so-called Triple-A supply chain[4] (see Box 1.1).

Box 1.1: A Closer Look at Triple-A Supply Chains

Hau Lee's research[5] into private sector companies shows that cost efficiency and speed are not sufficient. The key to a competitive supply chain is to extend the concern about cost efficiency and speed further to include agility, adaptability, and alignment – the three As.

Agility is the ability to quickly respond to short-term changes in demand or supply to handle external disruptions. This is the very nature of humanitarian

---

Box 1.1: (Continued)

supply chains where the time cycles are very short, new and unprecedented demands occur frequently, and external factors place physical, if not political or financial, constraints on the system.

Adaptability is the ability to adjust the supply chain design to meet the structural shifts in markets and modify supply network strategies, products, and technologies. As disasters, by definition, create flux within societies, structural and physical shifts are expected and desired for rehabilitation to start. Therefore humanitarian supply chains are designed to be, above all, adaptable to the environments in which they operate.

Alignment creates conditions for better performance and requires exchanging information with all relevant partners (vendors to consumers). It defines as well the responsibilities of all stakeholders to create a sense of unity and identity including aligned incentives. This presents the biggest challenge for any humanitarian supply chain (there is opportunity to learn from the private sector which is better at it).

Management Quality

Supply chain management performance is the result of a coherent end-to-end business model, an organizational design consistent with that business model, and flawless execution of the different types of flows. This is what we refer to as management quality, that is the capability of a team to manage the system accordingly. Achieving this level of coherence can be difficult in the humanitarian context as the following section explains.

CHARACTERISTICS OF A HUMANITARIAN SUPPLY CHAIN

Ambiguous Objectives

It is difficult to assess the level of commitment of the different actors and their relationship to one another, as the operations typically roll out with large numbers of stakeholders (donors, agencies, media, and beneficiaries). Actions in the humanitarian world are often uncoordinated, spontaneous, unsolicited, and disparate. The absence of a profit-making incentive, which is replaced here with the need for a speedy and lifesaving response, can lead to ad hoc firefighting behavior, as well as to frequent reinvention of the wheel (see Chapter 6).

Limited Resources

These are mixed with asymmetric investment of the different actors.

- *Human*: High turnover, heavy physical and emotional demands, limited pool of qualified and readily deployable personnel.
- *Capital*: Funds are not always available on time. Even when pledged they come after assessments and are not always paid on the spot. Liquidity, as well as good credit terms for new suppliers, is an issue for managers on the ground.

- *Infrastructure*: Often damaged by disasters, inexistent or insufficient for the magnitude of the needs since the emergency typically brings a peak in demand rarely seen in the areas affected.

High Uncertainty

Dependence on assessments and dynamic changes in supply and demand, mixed with a significant inability to assess the quality and quantity of assets other actors will contribute to the operation. Every disaster brings together a new set of actors with different resources and commitment level.

Urgency

Humanitarian interventions after a disaster are typically characterized by an acute urgency. This gives these operations a high level of intensity (where intensity can be measured by the number of tasks to be executed divided by the product of time and available resources).

Politicized Environment

Humanitarian operations are highly political throughout the supply chain, from donations to distribution in the field. It is quite difficult to maintain and protect a so-called humanitarian space in which humanitarians can do their relief job independently from outside pressures. Humanitarian space will be further explained in Chapter 2.

SPEED

Typically, industrial supply chains are evaluated using indicators like cost, speed, quality, and flexibility. While supply chains in various industries may focus on different indicators at different stages of their life cycle, humanitarian supply chains (for acute emergencies) have a more hierarchical set of changing performance indicators over time with the overriding objective at the start being speed. Indeed, after a sudden-onset disaster, speed of reaction is of the utmost importance in the first 72 hours in order to save a maximum of human lives.

With speed as the main driver, lead time reduction becomes an important area of consideration. Looking at the industries that compete on the basis of speed, research shows that the total lead time (the elapsed time to complete a business process) only contains 3–5 percent value adding time.[6] That leaves much room for improvement, especially in the humanitarian sector, where it can be assumed that supply chain operations are less mature than in the private sector. Of course any improvement in the supply chain lead time can have a significant positive impact on the beneficiaries (and therefore higher return on donations). This validates our focus on logistics as a key factor in the overall effectiveness of any humanitarian response.

Examples where humanitarian supply chains have long lead times and corresponding opportunities for reduction are as follows:

- Humanitarian aid often gets delayed in customs or at a warehouse while transportation is sought or the road is debottlenecked (waiting).

11

- Excessive controls lead to slow procedures at warehouses to receive or dispatch goods, and bureaucratic processes, for example in the UN system can provoke significant delays.
- In environments where things happen so fast, actors sometimes do not fully understand their impact on the rest of the supply chain (ambiguous goals and objectives).
- Collaboration is mostly relatively poor, again leading to delays in handovers.

OPPORTUNITIES FOR CROSS-LEARNING

Research[7] shows that there are two types of risks for commercial supply chains: disruption and coordination risks. How these risks are dealt with in the humanitarian supply chain can provide valuable lessons to the private sector.

Risk 1

This encompasses disruptions that result as global supply chains become more complex and geographically dispersed.

Complexity and dispersion are two fundamental characteristics of humanitarian supply chains. Relief operations can take place anywhere, any day, and affect any number of people. It is never immediately clear who should contribute what to fulfill the needs, for example to what extent can the UN or the Red Cross help, are the local military forces equipped for the task, how much local infrastructure has been destroyed? The needs are constantly changing, demanding high degrees of agility (e.g., 20,000 blankets are needed instead of 10,000) and adaptability (e.g., the main road has been destroyed overnight, we need to find an alternative route) from all parties. A lot of operations take place in areas where the crisis is still evolving (earthquakes have aftershocks, cyclones bring floods, civil unrest or attacks can erupt quickly and unexpectedly), so the supply chain is subject to new challenges every day.

Risk 2

This covers coordination risks of matching supply and demand under the inherent pressures of cost-conscious lean and leaner designs.

Since speed, not cost, is the critical driver for humanitarians, they face stringent pressures and challenges when it comes to matching supply and demand. In the humanitarian sector, demand is for the most part unknown. Until the first post-disaster assessments are made it is very difficult to know the needs on the ground. Experience can help agencies judge some of the basic essential items and their quantities needed, based on the region and estimated impact of the disaster. Still, disasters unfold in many directions, so demand changes rapidly, oftentimes peaking suddenly at speeds and magnitudes higher than the international community can absorb.

On the other hand, supply is almost always limited. Goods need to meet standards agreed to by the agencies, and for some of these goods the number of producers is very limited, with limited capacity (e.g., in 2005, worldwide supply for mosquito nets was lesser than demand). Even when goods can be sourced, lead times can be highly unpredictable. Resource planning in most emergency cases is very short-term or inexistent. This is all the more difficult when there is little possibility to analyze trends and no visibility in the pipeline (humanitarian supply chains frequently lack suitable information management systems).

Commercial supply chains in today's global competition aim to be agile, aligned, and adaptable. It is not just cost and speed that build a supply chain's competitive advantage. In the humanitarian world, the circumstances and settings are very different. Yet, they present attractive learning opportunities for private sector partners. For example, companies increasingly need the same skill sets as humanitarian relief organizations, given the dynamic demands and disruption risks of operating global supply chains, and the central role of logistics in making profits under these conditions. Many corporations have already incurred substantial financial losses due to their inability to respond to short-term changes in demand or supply (agility), or their slowness in adjusting designs to market changes (adaptability). As a result, corporations have realized that while high speed and low cost are necessary for a successful supply chain, they are not sufficient to give companies a competitive and sustainable advantage over rivals. Such advantage comes only when the supply chain is agile, adaptable, aligned, and resilient to disruptions.

Unlike the private sector, humanitarian organizations are specialists at being agile and adaptable, implementing complex supply chains under high levels of uncertainty with limited resources and infrastructure – and often overnight. For example, David Kaatrud, former Chief of Logistics for UNJLC, explains that in comparison to the private sector *"Our operational settings are typically very different and difficult. To get supplies to the most remote areas, we may have to resort to a range of imaginative and unconventional delivery systems, from air-dropping to using elephants for transport."*

Between disasters, alignment as an aspect of preparedness is an area in which the private sector is ready to transfer much knowledge and expertise to the humanitarian sector. The private sector has long focused on improving its supply chain by strengthening relationships with its partners and establishing incentives to improve the performance of the whole supply chain. This includes working between disasters to negotiate agreements with suppliers and service providers, and implementing tools that can provide greater visibility, facilitate communications and reporting, and enable better planning and forecasting.

SHARING KNOWLEDGE BETWEEN THE PRIVATE AND THE HUMANITARIAN SECTOR

Throughout this book we will be exploring the differences and similarities between the humanitarian and the private supply chains. Both sectors have a lot to learn from each other. In coming chapters we will discuss engagement models and frameworks for knowledge transfers. However, transfer of knowledge or best practices does not happen automatically. It actually requires a difficult process that needs to be managed proactively by the parties involved in order to be successful. Through our work with different organizations we have learned to recognize some of the barriers to best practice transfer and cross-learning. We discuss them in the rest of this book and suggest some actions to remove these barriers.

CONCLUSION

The evolution from logistics to supply chain management means that many more actors are responsible today for the final customer experience (cost, speed, price, etc.). In an effort to improve the final outcome, organizations allocate resources to manage their information, material and financial flows, as well as the skill set of their staff. For humanitarians this effort is more complicated given the context and the conditions in which they operate. As a result they have become more agile and adaptable than their private sector counterparts.

In return the private sector has managed to excel at alignment by focusing on the interaction between the numerous players in their supply chains, and by developing appropriate information and communication technology platforms. In addition, private sector actors are held together by a profit/loss logic prescribed in the business plan, rather than by humanitarian values and missions.

In their respective context, the humanitarian and private supply chain aim to excel, reducing the risks of disruptions and improving supply/demand coordination. Our work proposes that both supply chains can learn a lot from each other and become more competitive through the exchange of their best practices. In Chapter 7 we will focus on how the private and humanitarian sectors can learn from each other through public–private partnerships.

2

HUMANITARIANISM

INTRODUCTION

In Chapter 1 we discussed the key points of logistics and supply chain management as they apply to the humanitarian sector. In this chapter we discuss the key points of the literature from the humanitarian sector that we have used to build our work. In particular, this chapter presents the principles of humanity, neutrality, and impartiality; explains how these principles serve to shape the humanitarian space; and highlights the importance and challenge of operating within it.

NOT ALL THAT GLITTERS IS GOLD

When former UN High Commissioner for Refugees (UNHCR) Sadako Ogata suddenly suspended all UNHCR activities in Serbian-controlled Bosnia and withdrew most of its staff on 17 February 1993, the international community was in shock. Her decision was immediately condemned as being non-humanitarian by the Security Council. For days she was heavily criticized by her peers. Former Secretary General Boutros Boutros-Ghali reminded Ogata that political negotiations were underway in New York and highlighted that no decision over aid suspension should be regarded as purely operational in view of the greater political sensitivities involved.

While the Secretary General had valid points, Ogata's proximity to the realities of the field helped her to understand the political impact of the humanitarian operation. She forecasted that continuing the activities as they were would endanger the lives of her staff as well as those of the beneficiaries. She rightly accused the local political leaders of making a mockery of her efforts by not ensuring the safe passage of humanitarian assistance through their territory and blocking access to underserved groups. A few days later, when negotiations resumed, the situation changed positively. Safer conditions were created for her staff and humanitarian operations restarted properly, saving the lives of many neglected Muslims in the eastern enclaves. Bosnian Vice President Ejup Ganic personally thanked her for her hard-line, as did other political leaders and the media.[1]

The case in Serbian-controlled Bosnia highlights the conundrum that not all seemingly humanitarian solutions are as humanitarian as they first seem if we consider their long-term impact. Continuing with the status quo in Bosnia in 1993 would have compromised Ogata's mandate to save lives by actually putting more lives in danger.

In retrospect, we may underestimate the difficulty of her brave decision. It required a great understanding of the link between the local relief operations in the Balkans and the larger political process a continent away in New York. It took an understanding of the short-term versus the long-term impact of her decision. Stopping the operations may have had a negative impact on the conditions of the locals in the short run but the long-term effect was to reduce the number of victims and suffering. Despite the pressures, Ogata kept a clear focus on her long-term humanitarian mandate, which she says was the driving force behind her vision and decision.

Unfortunately, this type of visionary judgment is rarely possible in humanitarian interventions. Most crises are plagued by limited reliable information, an overwhelming sense of urgency, and local complexities that keep communication between political and humanitarian leaders at superficial levels. The unwanted element of surprise is forever lurking.

Consider the 2002 famine in Southern Africa. Several Southern African Developing Community (SADC) countries, many of whom were generally food self-sufficient, were at severe risk of starvation. Experts were claiming that an immediate supply of 1.2 million metric tons of food was needed, while an additional 4 million tons would be required over the next year.

The UN World Food Program (WFP) was the lead agency in the relief effort. The WFP worked with local emergency government boards to organize appeals and facilitate the arrival of support. The immediate crisis was compounded by unprecedented levels of HIV in the population, a regional economic downturn, diminishing national grain reserves, and limited access to scattered at-risk population. In summary, this was a complex crisis with strong political, economic, and demographic components interacting.

Logistically everything seemed to be in place. The ports, trains, and roads were assessed and reinforced; agreements with suppliers were negotiated and signed; transportation and warehousing were all coordinated, and the amounts of aid per region were allocated. However, the crisis took a significant turn as the aid began to arrive. The maize was found to be genetically modified, and in the eyes of Zambian authorities this was unacceptable. Zambian President Levy Mwanawasa voiced his opinion to the international community saying, *"Just because our people are hungry it doesn't mean we will feed them poison."*

All distribution of maize was temporarily suspended and WFP had to find an alternative solution to conduct their lifesaving mandate. The rejected maize had to be collected, and in some cases milled for redistribution. New sources of maize had to be identified and coordinated, sometimes at a premium price.

The Southern African food crisis is an example of the fact that even in dire emergencies there are rules and conditions that humanitarian assistance and donors must meet and that human suffering is not a green light for any type of action, regardless of the good intentions. For better or for worse, these examples show that humanitarian intervention is subject to political forces, and so this chapter begins by asking the question "Who has the final word on what is really humanitarian?" or, better yet, "What is humanitarian after all?"[2]

DEFINING "HUMANITARIAN"

While there are many interpretations of what is or could be considered to be a humanitarian action, three widely accepted principles – humanity, neutrality, and impartiality – must be present to constitute a humanitarian operation. These principles were developed by Henry Dunant after the battle of Solferino (1859), initially to protect the rights of soldiers. In 1864 they became part of the Geneva Convention, and in 1875 were the seeds for the Red

Cross Movement. These principles should be observed by humanitarians in their decision-making, as shown in the UNHCR and WFP examples earlier in this chapter. Widely shared by most organizations, they form part of today's policy that sets the parameters for action, and delineates the roles of agencies.

Humanity

This implies that human suffering should be relieved wherever found. It is the very reason why humanitarian organizations are deployed. Keeping in mind that in order to relieve suffering, humanitarian assistance brings scarce resources into societies affected by disaster and often experiencing social change, where the process of change itself often involves conflict.[3]

One challenge for agencies is to identify and access groups in need. In the Balkans, the UNHCR understood the needs in the region and had resources there to help, but there were problems of access due to security and fighting which restricted its ability to serve victims equitably.

Regardless of security, the neediest areas tend to be the most underdeveloped and thus the hardest to access. For example, in the case of the isolated populations of eastern Mozambique during the 2002 Southern African food crisis, it was not until after implementation had begun that aid agencies discovered that these relatively remote groups, far from the capital Maputo, were the hardest hit. Given their proximity to national borders, these groups had traditionally relied on the informal interaction with markets in neighboring countries. When trade restrictions were imposed due to the differing positions among

countries on the distribution of the genetically modified relief maize, these groups suffered more than those
that relied on markets within their own countries. Before
the relief program could be implemented, information
about them was simply not available because they were
difficult to access and had little contact with the national
authorities.

Neutrality

This implies that relief should be provided without bias or
affiliation to a party in the conflict. On the basis of neutrality, agencies may choose not to participate in local issues
if there is an eminent risk of getting trapped by political
agendas.

Maintaining a neutral stance is perhaps the most challenging and costly condition for agencies. The cost of
neutrality for WFP was rather high during the Southern
African food crisis of 2002. On the basis of neutrality, WFP
was forced to remove all genetically engineered relief maize
from Zambian territory and suspend its distribution.

To fulfill the urgent needs, WFP negotiated a series of
local solutions through its regional offices. WFP redesigned
the entire distribution and purchasing strategy, and bro-
kered agreements to reopen mothballed mills to grind the
genetically modified maize, which would prevent it from
being replanted or fed to livestock. Then, it had to find
new and readily accessible donors to supply new food
and cover transportation costs. Lastly, it began the largest
cash procurement operation in that region's history, buying
small quantities of food in markets throughout the region.
The operation became much more complex than WFP had
envisioned.

Impartiality

This indicates that assistance should be provided without discrimination and with priority given to the most urgent needs. Impartiality in operations can be evaluated more precisely in terms of non-discrimination between groups, proportionality in relation to need, and non-subjective recognition of needs as identified by the community.[4]

In Ogata's Bosnian case study, the desire to maintain impartiality was the issue behind the suspension of assistance. Failure to stop operations would have meant the neglect of Muslim communities in the eastern enclaves of Serbian-controlled Bosnia. In this case, the Serbian refusal to allow access to Muslim communities undermined UNHCR's capacity to be impartial, and thus risked skewing the benefits in function of the political agendas of the belligerents (see Box 2.1[5]).

Box 2.1: Humanitarian Ideologies

While the principles of humanity, neutrality, and impartiality are universal, aid agencies have different interpretations of their own mandate within the parameters of the principles. Some are adapted to their sector of activity like water, medicine, or children but at the base they still embody the same concepts spelled out by the three principles.

However, differences are noted based on the founding ideologies of the organizations. We can group agencies into three traditions based on these ideologies:

Box 2.1: (Continued)

1. *Faith-based organizations*, where faith-based work combines religious values with social goals. However, even though they are faith-based, they are ecumenical and do not impose their values on the beneficiaries they serve. Examples of these organizations include Catholic Relief Services and Caritas.

2. *Dunantists*, whose beliefs are firmly rooted in the principles advocated by Henry Dunant, who, as described earlier, launched the Red Cross Movement in 1875. They have worked tirelessly to uphold the principles of impartiality and neutrality and advocate a non-interventionist strategy in conflict. In addition to the Red Cross and Crescent Movement, this group also includes Oxfam, Save the Children, Médecins Sans Frontières (Doctors Without Borders), and Action Contre la Faim (Action Against Hunger).

3. *Wilsonians* with roots firmly planted in politics. They encompass former President Woodrow Wilson's ambitions to project US values and influence as a force for good in the world. Although it started out as a US movement, first seen in action throughout the Marshall Plan, it now spans the whole political spectrum (e.g., Cooperative for American Remittances to Europe (CARE), founded after WWII to deliver US Army food parcels surplus during the Marshall Plan). Wilsonians and faith-based organizations could be said to have

a built-in conflict of interest depending on how much their ideologies influence their agenda (political or religious).

HUMANITARIAN SPACE

Driven by the three principles, UNHCR and WFP responded to a changing environment in both case studies. The principles were not goals in themselves, but rather a framework or a means to an end. What the organizations aimed to create was a space in which they could properly conduct humanitarian work.

Establishing and maintaining this humanitarian space is a difficult task as the examples showed. Both agencies had their space reduced, one by security issues (Bosnia) and the other by political restrictions (Zambia). Difficulty arises because the space is dynamic and changes rapidly based on the conditions in the field (e.g., security could limit access to certain areas and weather conditions can have the same effect in natural disasters). Another challenging component of humanitarian space is that it is defined by non-humanitarian actors (e.g., governments, belligerents, military) based on their understanding and priorities, which are not always necessarily philanthropic or motivated by humanitarian principles.

Physical and Virtual

Humanitarian space exists in a physical (Bosnia) and a virtual sense (Zambia), and it is the goal of all humanitarians to live and operate within it. In the physical sense, humanitarian space represents a zone where civilians, non-combatants and aid workers are protected from violence and attack and can move and operate freely. The primary concern for preserving the physical space is security and access, as was the case in the Balkans.

For political conflicts, it is difficult to establish humanitarian space particularly in the absence of an effective government (e.g., Afghanistan, Iraq), when the present government is part of the conflict (e.g., Balkans, or Sudan), or when the local government requests humanitarian assistance on its terms (e.g., SADC countries in the Southern African food crisis). It also becomes an issue when the protagonists no longer believe that war has limits and begin to manipulate and change the humanitarian space for their own ends.

In the virtual sense, humanitarian space represents the interaction between the different members of the humanitarian ecosystem, and how they create an environment where their mandates can be executed. Sticking to humanitarian principles in complex environments is often very difficult as in the Southern African famine case, where prohibition of genetically modified maize affected relief efforts.

For natural disasters, humanitarian space is an important issue. However, in natural disasters humanitarian space tends to be easier to define as the government and different parties often share baseline goals. In such a case, it becomes a matter of setting the rules for an effective logistics operation in the virtual interpretation of the space.

Figure 2.1 gives a visual interpretation of this concept, where we refer to the area within the triangle as the humanitarian space. Note that the principles form an equilateral

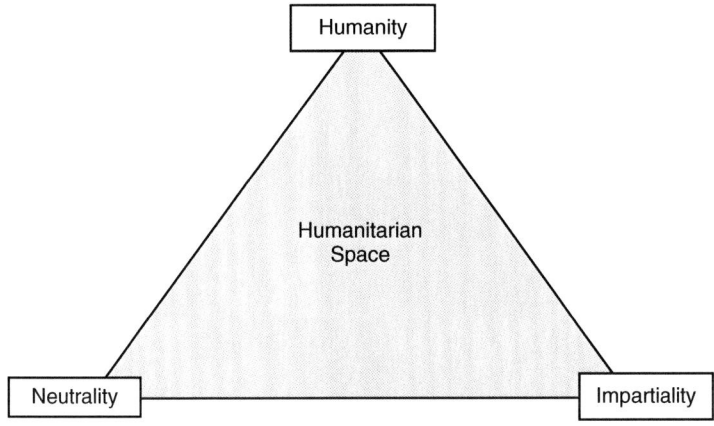

FIGURE 2.1 **Humanitarian Space and Principles**

triangle (since all three principles are of equal weight). Maintaining its balance is what agencies strive for. Any compromise on a principle would affect the size and shape of the triangle, affecting the outcome of the crisis and the agencies' ability to operate.

CONFLICT CONNECTION

As challenging as it may seem, agencies constantly invest resources in maintaining the humanitarian space, regardless of the time and effort. For WFP, it translated into a substantial change in their regional pipelines in Southern Africa demanding a significantly higher budget and, much like the Bosnian case, creating delays. So, what is outside the triangle that agencies should avoid so much?

Every crisis has the same actors (UN, NGOs, Red Cross, government, military, insurgent groups) in a continuing effort to find a solution to recurring problems: obstruction of humanitarian access; manipulation of relief; inequitable

TABLE 2.1 **Spectrum of Humanitarians (Inspired by MacFarlane's work)**

Position	Aim	Connection
Classical Humanitarian	• Full adherence to humanitarian principles. Seeks to assist regardless of the consequences.	• Failure to consider consequences of aid runs the risk of politicization of assistance.
Damage Limitation	• Avoid doing harm in the process of providing assistance and protection.	• Compromises neutrality and impartiality, replacing them with political objectives and shaping the process of conflict.
Conflict Transformation	• The use of humanitarian action to promote peace only.	
Aid for Victory	• The use of humanitarian action to secure the victory of one side over another.	• Aid as a weapon with no adherence to humanitarian principles.

28

economic relationships; or the absence of viable local structures.[6] In the process, when the aid favors one side over the others and/or changes the outcome of a political situation, the aid is said to be inflicting conflict.

The conflict connection happens when the humanitarian intervention disregards the boundaries set by humanitarian principles. The principles set a limit to prevent the humanitarian aid from interfering in the outcome of a conflict by strengthening any of the parties[7] (see Table 2.1). For example, any compromise on the humanity principle, such as using aid to secure the victory of one side over another, would nullify the intent of the operation taking it out of the ethical context and mandate of the participating organizations.

The conflict can take many shapes or be driven by different objectives. Often, decisions at the local, regional, or international levels are taken to transform aid (perhaps unintended) into a tool for damage limitation, or a tool to transform a conflict. In either case, political objectives are compromising the work of the agencies for a non-humanitarian outcome. Less frequently is the case where agencies are manipulated to favor one party exclusively in which case the intervention has lost its humanitarian purpose.

THE HUMANITARIAN CHALLENGE

Maintaining humanitarian space can, in practice, be enormously difficult. Key challenges we have identified in our research include ambiguous goals, impact, levels of influence, political–humanitarian relations, funding, willingness, and consent.

Ambiguous Goals

As agencies struggle to maintain the humanitarian space, operationalizing the three principles can often be ambiguous. To illustrate the problem let us analyze the following hypothetical example.

Consider a situation where an inventory manager is responsible for allocating aid between two camps hosting two opposing parties in conflict. The first camp is only a short travel distance from the warehouse, while the second camp is twice as far and the needs are greater. He has received his total stock of aid for one week, and the quantity does not cover the combined needs of the two camps.

Should the inventory manager decide to follow the principle of humanity, he would distribute his total stock of aid to the largest number of people. That is, he would give it all to the nearest camp, where travel distance is shorter. By doing so, however, he would ignore the needs of the second camp and compromise the neutrality and impartiality of the operation.

Alternatively, suppose he decides to follow the principle of impartiality and distribute the total stock to yield the greatest benefit. In this case he sends all the aid to the second, and farther, camp where the needs are greater. By doing so, he compromises the principles of humanity and neutrality in the operation.

Finally, suppose that to be neutral he decides to share the aid between the two camps. To avoid compromising the other principles he must share the aid keeping in mind the difference in travel distance and demand so that both camps receive aid proportionately related to their needs and location.

As the space is dynamic (shape of the triangle changes), agencies will prioritize different principles at different points depending on the information they have about the conditions of the beneficiaries and of the route. This demands that agencies be very flexible throughout the different stages of the response to adapt to alternating priorities and maintain the space (and push the corners of the triangle as needed).

Impact

The ambiguous goals discussions lead us to the question of impact. How is impact measured in humanitarian operations? How can we tell the impact of logistical decisions?

Many political issues and concepts relevant to emergencies are hard to quantify. There are long debates about what indicators are representative of "protection to civilians" or "risk reduction," at what level they should be measured, and to whom the measurement is relevant and useful. Where quantification is possible, considering the myriad of factors interacting in an emergency and how little may be known about the dynamics of the locals prior to the emergency, there are usually issues about the lack of baseline data and problems of attribution.[8]

For field-based and process-oriented activities like logistics, it is easier to build and agree on indicators for efficiency and effectiveness (e.g., cost, delivery time, quality). These indicators are helpful to identify room for improvement as well as to pinpoint areas in which collaboration with other agencies could be useful to optimize resources. For example, UNICEF is well known for its procurement capabilities and WFP for its logistics and distribution.

However, these quantifiable field-based indicators (speed and cost) are not enough. They fail to provide a full picture of the ecosystem, thus reducing the humanitarian intervention to a technical scale.[9] The challenge remains how to link the quantifiable (oftentimes operational) indicators with the qualitative (oftentimes socio-political) so that they can alert agencies in the field to the non-humanitarian effects of their actions.

Even when this reconciliation is possible, there is a limitation due to the time frame. Logistics provides short-term results for short-term needs. However, any kind of humanitarian aid has a long-term impact on a changing environment whose future is hard to predict. It is difficult to know for the long run how a single humanitarian action (like providing relief aid or food to the Hutus or the Tutsis in Rwanda) will interact with the political, social, and economic factors contributing to the long-term outcome of the crisis.

Levels of Influence

At what level (local, regional, or international) should aid impact be measured? Part of the challenge of maintaining humanitarian space is that it is shaped at different levels with local, regional, and international bodies and situations contributing to the chaos. So the triangle of Figure 2.1 representing humanitarian space effectively becomes a pyramid where the humanitarian principles need to be balanced at the interconnected levels (see Figure 2.2).

During an emergency operation the pyramid builds from the bottom up with the needs on the ground driving the agenda. Assessments of population needs help to determine the size and magnitude of the operation to generate

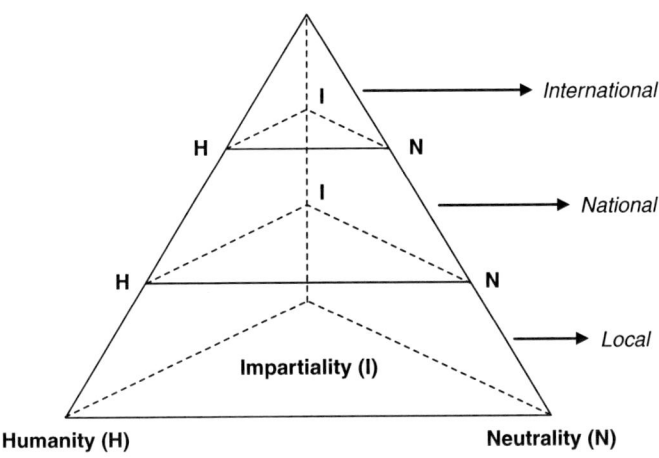

FIGURE 2.2 **Different Levels of Influence**

appeals as was the case in the Southern African food crisis of 2002.

We believe local conditions are the foundation since they are the closest to implementation and it is where logistical bottlenecks will have the greatest impact on the operation. Issues of security, access to population or information are some of the tools that local actors may use to manipulate access to limited resources (e.g., humanitarian aid, infrastructure, telecommunications, warehouse, and transport), and impose their political agendas. For example, in the Balkans, deteriorating security blocked access to regions where needs were high.

At the regional level, the reaction of governments and semi-government bodies contributes to operating conditions as well. In Southern Africa, WFP implemented a regional office that liaised with the SADC and other governmental entities to facilitate the dialogue between the countries. This proved very helpful when the genetically modified maize was rejected. The collaboration between governments, fostered by the regional WFP office which had a solid understanding of the complexity of the crisis, was crucial to reaching a solution.

On the other hand, regional agendas can be counterproductive. During conflicts, governments affected by instability have important political interests vested in the outcomes of nearby conflicts, and can regulate the evolution of the conflict to affect the outcome.

Lastly, the international community plays a significant role. Much criticism has arisen concerning the crisis in Darfur, Sudan, with the UN Security Council and the international community coming under fire for failing to raise the profile of the region, thus delaying much needed help. While political action at varying levels opens the door for humanitarian intervention, sovereign states have the right to refuse international aid (e.g., India during the Indian Ocean tsunami). No UN agency or humanitarian organization can impose themselves on a sovereign state (except when genocide is confirmed).

The shape of the triangle varies at different stages. During preliminary negotiations, we find that all the power and energy is concentrated at the top, with nothing happening at the bottom; for example, Southern Sudan before the peace treaty between the Muslim north and the Christian and animist south was signed in January 2005, and Iraq before the US/international intervention. In these cases none of the field operations were active, and the triangle could take many shapes. Likewise, some crises never rise to the top, having been solved at the local level, or others never get to the implementation stage with all the energy in political efforts alone.

Political–Humanitarian Relations

Politics at any level play an important role in defining the humanitarian space. UNHCR's Ogata, from her personal experience in Bosnia claimed that *"There are no humanitarian solutions to humanitarian problems.... Humanitarian assistance ameliorates suffering to bridge victims over periods of time but on its own could never reach a solution."*[10] Her expression is a call to understand that humanitarian intervention is closely linked with the political process. Living isolated from politics is almost impossible. Still, the intervention must prevent political considerations from skewing and outweighing the humanitarian objectives. Politics are constantly shaping the space and the operational conditions.

Funding

This is, without a doubt, the most sensitive link between politics and humanitarian intervention. Regarding funding and principles, the International Federation of the Red Cross highlights in its 2003 annual report[11] that human suffering around the world is largely ignored unless political considerations overlap with the humanitarian ones. As a result of this favoritism by donors, funds are not necessarily proportional to needs, and giving is, for the most part, prioritized by donors' political agendas. The Red Cross points out that funds tend to be allocated for visible and high profile issues rather than on a needs basis. Many times, the highest and most urgent needs go unnoticed when the media fails to expose them.

Inevitably, mediatization of a crisis has a direct impact on fund-raising. The downside is that many crises are fatigued, forgotten, or off the radar of many news providers. With so many competing headlines, the sensational ones are more attractive and thus the media chooses carefully what they can sell at different points. Crises and emergencies do not happen in linear fashion; many happen simultaneously and compete for airtime and attention.

As a result, not only do the more urgent needs get bypassed, but so does funding for prevention and long-term development. Donors tend to be more responsive to short-term needs and emergencies, rather than preventive and long-term measures that would minimize the likelihood of crises or aid dependency (e.g., Afghanistan).

Even when they are allocated, funds come with strings attached. Donors can earmark donations and influence the way they are spent. Earmarking donations is a tool that donors can use to target their investment in particular areas or sectors. Earmarking forces agencies to spend according to the donors' priorities and not necessarily to the highest ranking needs in the field. As such, humanitarians enter into a service provider relation with the donor that undermines their legitimacy in some cases.

For example, a government can request that goods be bought and/or transported from their national industries or overseas investments. They can also express their desire to have the aid only in the form of food produced in their region (while the primary need may be medicine), or medicines produced in their labs (that are more expensive to send in comparison with local providers).

Earmarked donations are restrictive in the sense that they can be used only for their original purpose. This may be for a specific disaster, while other, newer emergencies are underserved. In the aftermath of the Indian Ocean tsunami, the French relief organization Médecins Sans

Frontières (MSF) asked donors not to send more money for the tsunami relief and reminded them about other urgent needs in the world, neglected by the media. There may also be internal needs for humanitarian organizations such as training, new equipment, more personnel, and so on.

Willingness and Consent

The relationship between the political and the humanitarian sector is difficult and complex. It is easy in hindsight to criticize negative outcomes, but we would like to believe that for the most part the initial intentions of all parties are altruistic.

So why or where do good intentions go wrong? Focusing again on the operations theater, we could evaluate the position of the different players in terms of their willingness to help and their level of consent. The framework we present[12] in Figure 2.3 helps us understand the needs and limitations for a political–humanitarian relationship.

In the first quadrant parties are willing and able to collaborate to meet the needs. This reduces the likelihood of

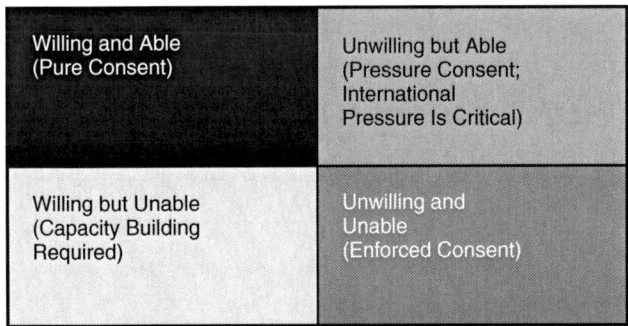

FIGURE 2.3 **Willingness and Consent**

conflict connection and facilitates inter-agency collaboration in the field. A hypothetical example: if Zambia had accepted the genetically modified maize. This quadrant is rare, since it is built on conditions rarely present in conflict areas or heavily politicized environments.

In the second quadrant, the parties involved are unwilling but able to play their role in the humanitarian intervention. We could say this was the case of the Balkans in the Ogata example, or the case of Zambia vis-à-vis the genetically engineered maize. In this case international pressure is needed to ensure cooperation and minimize the risk of a conflict connection for the aid.

In the third quadrant, the parties are willing but unable to play their roles in a humanitarian way. For these countries capacity building is required since the limitations are primarily technical or infrastructural. An example is WFP assisting SADC countries to mill the maize by reopening mothballed establishments.

Lastly, in the fourth quadrant, when players are unwilling and unable, bottlenecks are introduced at all levels. For these, a comprehensive plan needs to be developed for assistance where political pressure is coupled with humanitarian aid and capacity building. We could argue this is the case of genocide.

CONCLUSION

Humanitarian decisions demand a combination of good understanding of the field and operational needs, as well as the political setting. This combination can be made difficult by the complexity of settings and the short-term visibility of the factors that can affect the situation. What at times may seem like the best solution may in the long run turn out to be the worst or most difficult.

Unlike commercial supply chains, humanitarian operations are not judged by their speed or costs, but rather by their impact. This means adhering to the humanitarian principles at all cost, which at times can prove to be very expensive (e.g., Southern Africa), or controversial (e.g., the Balkans).

Humanitarian workers face the challenge of finding neutral ways to operationalize their mandate without compromising the principles or producing negative impact. They also need to anticipate and minimize the impact of manipulation of aid and avoid conflict through constant dialogue with the different parties. For example, when making local purchases should ensure local economies are not perturbed, or when choosing a transportation provider or route should not strengthen one group over another.

In subsequent chapters we will be building upon the humanitarian principles discussed here to better understand their implications when making decisions on the ground. Numerous examples will show how difficult it can be at times to build and maintain the humanitarian space.

3

PREPAREDNESS

INTRODUCTION

In this chapter we discuss how, under the high uncertainties and complexities faced by humanitarian organizations, disaster management is the result of a long and structured process of strategic process design (preparedness) that ultimately drives successful execution (response).

HURRICANE MITCH

Between 22 October and 1 November 1998, Hurricane Mitch[1], a 180-mph Category 5 storm, the worst to hit the Gulf of Mexico in 200 years, swept through Central America devastating the economies of Honduras, Nicaragua, and Guatemala. The hurricane dumped as much as six feet of rain, washed out roads, destroyed some 400 bridges in the region, changed the course of rivers, and left a three-foot layer of mud on flooded airfields. An estimated 10,000 people died while some 2 million were left homeless. In January 1999, Honduras' President Carlos Flores stated, "We lost in 72 hours what had taken us more than 50 years to build, bit by bit."

As for the response of the International Federation of Red Cross and Red Crescent Societies (IFRC), nothing went right. It took weeks before IFRC took a lead in coordinating the relief contributions of the donating National Societies (NS). Technical staff and relief delegates arrived unreasonably late in the region. Emergency Response Units (ERUs) – which included specialized equipment and experts addressing logistics, health (basic healthcare and referral hospitals), telecommunications, and water and sanitation issues – were deployed too late from Geneva. It took weeks to mobilize and distribute basic supplies such as food, water, and shelter to the population.

The IFRC had been caught unprepared and failed to play a coordinating role in managing the disaster, mainly because IFRC staff arrived too late on the scene. When they did finally show up they were not sufficiently prepared to respond to the crisis. Not enough technical expertise was available for deployment, and relief supplies were slow in coming because of the IFRC's failure to consider prepositioning.

SUCCESSFUL RESPONSES ARE NOT IMPROVISED

Too often, humanitarian agencies find themselves in a situation described by disaster management literature as firefighting, where understaffed and underequipped agencies try their best but find that their solutions are incomplete, that problems recur and cascade, and urgency rather than overall importance is the critical driver. Eventually such firefighting agencies see their performance drop (see Box 3.1[2]).

Box 3.1: Stop Fighting Fires

Firefighting is common among organizations in every sector. People rush from one crisis to the next, never really fixing problems, just stopping them from getting worse. Firefighting is one of the most serious problems facing many managers of complex, change-driven processes, explains Bohn.

Firefighting is best characterized as a collection of symptoms. You are a victim if at least three of the following linked elements are chronic within your business unit or division:

- There is not enough time to solve all the problems.
- Solutions are incomplete.
- Problems recur and cascade.
- Urgency supersedes importance.
- Many problems become crises.
- Performance drops.

In one example, Bohn explains that at NASA some engineers were borrowed from other programs in the early phases of a particular project thus forcing their original programs to fall behind schedule. Engineers worked 70-hour weeks to meet deadlines, causing more errors in the short run and declines in effectiveness in the long run. Early warning signs were ignored or missed.

Firefighting is not necessarily disastrous. Clearly it hampers performance, but there are worse alternatives. Rigid bureaucratic rules, for example, can help a company avoid firefighting altogether, but at the price

---

Box 3.1: (Continued)

of almost no problems ever getting solved. At least firefighting lets agencies put out some small fires completely.

The Disaster Management Cycle

To better understand how firefighting can be avoided in disaster relief operations let us start by defining disaster management. The full cycle of disaster management includes four steps:

- *Mitigation*
- *Preparedness*
- *Response*
- *Rehabilitation*

Since the focus of this book is disaster logistics, we concentrate on the middle two steps – preparedness and response. The mitigation and rehabilitation phases fall outside our scope (see Figure 3.1 and Box 3.2).

For our purposes we define disaster management as a combination of preparedness and response. Preparedness addresses the strategy put in place that allows the implementation of a successful operational response in the theater.

The idea behind our disaster management definition is that preparedness becomes, in itself, a mini-cycle in which organizations are working not only during disasters but also between them, constantly learning and adapting to new challenges.

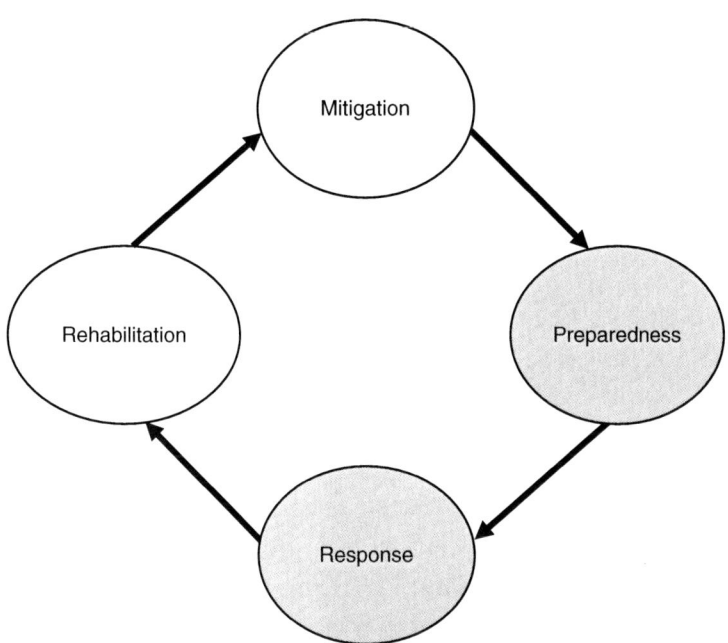

FIGURE 3.1 **Disaster Management Cycle**

Box 3.2: Full Cycle of Disasters

Mitigation addresses the proactive social component of emergencies. This includes laws and mechanisms that reduce the vulnerability of the population and increases their resilience. For example, building codes and restrictions will ensure that homes are built in areas where they are less prone to disasters while preventing them from causing one (e.g., a building on the edge of a cliff next to a river on muddy soil).

Preparedness will be discussed in great detail in this chapter. Basically it means putting in place the

Box 3.2: (Continued)

response mechanisms to counter factors that society has not been able to mitigate (withstanding risks and vulnerability). While the city may have building codes and regulations, which include fire safety, they cannot nullify the likelihood and the impact of a fire. Therefore cities have a fire department that will be prepared to attend to the need, should it arise.

Response (to continue with our fire example) is the act of attending to the fire. From a logistical point of view response during a disaster is very complex. Unlike logisticians in the private sector, humanitarians are faced with the unknown, not knowing where, when, and how big the next disaster will be. Even worse, they don't know how many people will be affected and for how long a time.

Responding is only the beginning. Accurate data for both demand and supply can be scarce during the course of a relief operation. Dealing with unexpected events also means humanitarians often have to pull out of one disaster and head off to another virtually overnight. Considering the difficult circumstances and the typical lack of resources, this puts extra pressure on people (high stress and turnover levels) and challenges an organization's capability to invest in learning and skills improvement.

Rehabilitation comes after the response, when society supported by surviving institutions and infrastructure seeks to restore some form of normality to the victims' lives. This is not simply a return to the status quo, since that was proven to be vulnerable to disaster. Rather, it should be an improvement – one that prevents or at least lessens the odds that those living in a burnt-out or destroyed building will lose their homes again.

Working between disasters means setting up processes, mechanisms, and even supplies that can be trusted to respond to the dynamic environment of disasters and support an agile, adaptable, and aligned response. For this to be the case, all the tools and mechanisms need to be accessible within the humanitarian ecosystem, but most important within the organizations themselves.

Later in this chapter we will use the IFRC case (see Table 3.2 and Figure 3.2) to demonstrate what we consider to be the five building blocks of preparedness.

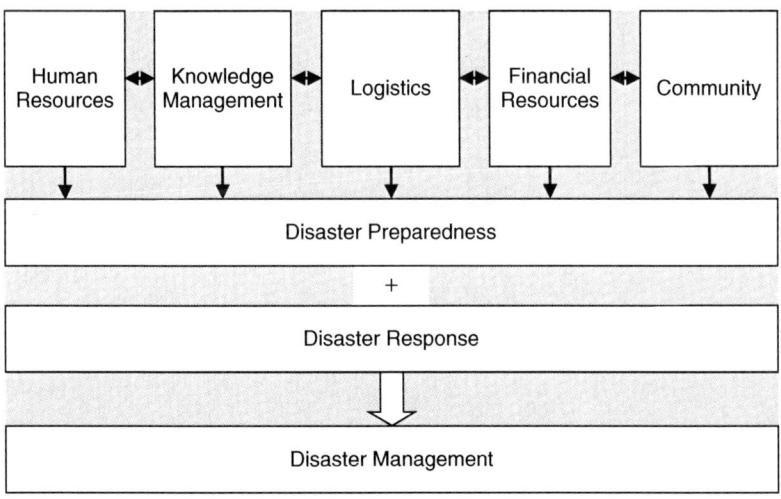

FIGURE 3.2 **Five Building Blocks of Preparedness**

PREPAREDNESS CHALLENGES

The onset of a disaster triggers cries of help that demand immediate response – the right goods, at the right time, to the right place, and distributed to the right people. As such, we can consider the onset of the disaster response (implementation of strategy when it exists) as the beginning of five essential flows we discussed in Chapter 1: materials, information, finance, people, and knowledge (see Table 3.1).

Materials

Because of the urgency and the high stakes involved, humanitarian agencies may be more comfortable assuming a premium to get the right goods to the right place at the right time. Early on in a disaster, goods may be flown in from abroad as quickly as possible, despite the expense. Later on (the first 90–100 days), the response becomes a mixture of being effective in helping victims and getting it done at a reasonable cost. At this stage, humanitarians might start looking at buying more relief goods locally.

TABLE 3.1 **Goals per Flow**

Flow	Goal
Material (Boxes)	• Cost, speed, and quality
Information (Bytes)	• Limited access, then overflow • Relevance: Tool for coordination
Funds (Bucks)	• Liquidity: Going from soft bids to cash • Needs-based prioritization
People (Bodies)	• Getting staff to the field
Knowledge (Brains)	• Making skills available to create solutions

Supply chain studies[3] show that significant amounts of time and resources (sometimes up to 95%) are wasted waiting for goods to arrive on the scene (at customs, in warehouses, etc.). In a field like disaster management, a reduction of this percentage could be turned into lives saved.

But not every type of good is needed in every disaster, and thus a lot of unsolicited donations may become a burden to the system. Therefore it is important that the flow of goods be monitored and communicated to improve efficiency and efficacy.

Information

Information is very limited at the beginning of a disaster, even if there were good assessments of the area prior to the calamity (which is rarely the case). Early in a disaster it is critical to understand the impact on specific areas and the needs surfacing at different levels. It is essential to design and coordinate the response. Information is critical in designing a supply chain that addresses the needs of the population (water, food, medicines, shelter) and defining the means to meet those needs (warehousing capacity, airport or corridor access, transport capabilities, telecommunications). Smooth coordination and avoidance of duplication of effort relies on information sharing, knowing who will be involved in the disaster response, in what capacity (lead agency, implementing partner, inter-agency coordinator, etc.). In Chapter 5 we discuss the challenges of information management in disasters in greater detail.

Funds

The compelling images emanating from disaster areas are critical to agency fund-raising efforts and the allocation of emergency funds. However, it is naïve to believe that this leads to an equitable distribution on a needs basis (see Chapter 5 for a discussion of transparency and accountability). In fact, only crises that have great media exposure are able to raise significant funds for an immediate response. Compounding the challenge is that the public is often quickly fatigued by repeated appeals or distracted by new crises, causing funds for a specific relief operation to dry up earlier than expected.

As IFRC notes in its World Disaster Report from 2003,[4] the hardest hit regions and populations are not always the ones receiving the aid. Numerous, and long-predicted, crises in Africa have had mixed results when appeals were made to the international community. Meanwhile other crises, where political considerations come into play, have been much more successful at raising funds. But even then, these funds are not necessarily a panacea. Funds that are not properly invested or dispersed can lead to aid dependency and hamper the long-term recovery prospects of the beneficiaries. Aid dependency means that rehabilitation may never start and agencies can be trapped in a self-perpetuating cycle with little chance of long-term sustainable recovery.

What is even more important in terms of disaster response fund-raising is liquidity. Most of the pledged funds will take days, weeks, perhaps even months or years to reach the agencies at a time when they need to finance their immediate operations with cash and meet financial obligations to their supply chain partners.

Finding funds to support disaster preparedness is difficult. Donations for a disaster are earmarked for relief and not for training and investment in preparedness strategies in between disasters. According to Bernard Chomilier, former Head of Logistics at the IFRC: *"It is easy to find resources to respond, it is hard to find resources to be more ready to respond."*

We must recognize that there are slow-onset and sudden-onset disasters. Slow-onset disasters are easier to prepare for in advance since time permits it. Experience shows the window of opportunity to raise funds is when the humanitarian needs overlap with media attention (which in itself is often driven by political agendas). Rarely is that window ever seen in a preparedness phase.

People

Getting the right skill sets to disaster areas is not an easy task either. First, these people need to be available for deployment. During the 2001 earthquakes in El Salvador, as in many other disasters, many of the locally trained staff could not assist as they were themselves victims of the earthquakes. Foreign teams often need to come in to assess and assist in the response. These newcomers will train local and foreign staff for the longer tasks while integrating volunteers at different levels. These expatriate specialists often leave on a moment's notice for the next crisis. People are also subject to burnout under high physical and emotional demands, working with limited resources in an intense environment.

Knowledge

Every disaster is an opportunity for knowledge transfer and capacity building. Specialized knowledge is required to make quick decisions under high uncertainty when designing a response. This is knowledge that could be already present in the area from the local emergency response teams, but also knowledge that may need to be imported. In most cases this knowledge is brought by the people that come to respond, but in some cases this knowledge may also be accessible through virtual networks via Internet, video, or conference calls, or simply repackaged into products sent to the area (see Chapter 6).

The type of knowledge needed changes at different points of the disaster demanding a variety of expertise to be available. In Chapter 4 we discuss the different stages of a disaster and how each one of them requires a different set of skills. Lastly, knowledge itself is created during a response and it is the responsibility of the organizations to capture that knowledge for future uses.

LOGISTICS BECOMES A CENTRAL FUNCTION FROM HURRICANE MITCH TO GUJARAT

A significant stumbling block to better preparedness in the humanitarian sector has been the failure to have logistics recognized as an essential element of any relief operation. It is argued that the response to most disasters is comprised of 80 percent logistics (considering number of activities, funds allocated, and skills required). The cases that follow show how IFRC came to that realization, changed focus to acknowledge logistics as a central function, and integrated it into their preparedness strategy.

Aware of its inefficiencies and facing criticism, in 2000 the IFRC commissioned a report from the consulting firm McKinsey & Company that initiated a restructuring exercise. The first significant change was to underline the clear distinction between ongoing development and disaster management (emergencies). This was achieved by creating two divisions: Knowledge Sharing, and Disaster Management and Coordination.

McKinsey also helped IFRC to recognize that logistics and supply chain management needed to be at the very heart of operations, raising the profile of logistics from mainly a back-office function to a department in its own right. This prompted the creation of the Logistics and Resource Mobilization Unit (RMU).

RMU became part of the Disaster Management and Coordination division that also included a new Emergency Response and Preparedness department and three Operations Managers responsible for coordinating emergencies on a global scale. Following the restructuring, the RMU was tasked with finding better and more efficient ways of getting the right funds, goods, and people mobilized and in place as fast as possible. This was quite a move away from the traditional logistics and resource mobilization activities that centered on a purely purchasing function.

By the time of the Gujarat earthquake (see Box 3.3[5]), IFRC had implemented preparedness initiatives that would allow faster responses than before. Their new strategy allowed the IFRC to effectively utilize all available resources at once, and be the first at the scene of the disaster. Indeed that was the goal of the new readily deployable mechanisms and tools including equipment and people, such as the Field Assessment Coordination Team (FACT), that the IFRC had lacked during Hurricane Mitch. The FACT team, which was on standby and deployable within 12–24 hours for a stay of up to 6 weeks anywhere in the world, was able to carry out rapid field assessment immediately after a disaster, ensure coordination with dozens of actors, and make quick decisions. There were also highly skilled, first-line relief operators who were part of the new

Regional Intervention Teams (RITs). Reports were generated and debriefing sessions held. Considerable efforts had gone into improving logistics systems, and frame agreements with international and local suppliers had been set up, enabling supplies to be distributed swiftly.

Box 3.3: IFRC Case Study – Gujarat Earthquake

On 26 January 2001, an earthquake measuring 7.9 on the Richter scale struck at 8.50 a.m. in Gujarat, on the west coast of India. It ravaged the country destroying five districts and killing over 20,000 people. Added to this devastation were the difficulties of working in a politically sensitive area, rife with local conflict and under heavy armed presence. Its close proximity to the Pakistani border was also not to be taken lightly.

When humanitarian organizations arrived on the scene they were faced with a high degree of uncertainty and lack of reliable information. For example, the actual death toll was probably closer to 50,000 than the official figure but nobody will ever know the exact numbers because of insufficient data. Lack of accurate data, coupled with the mass destruction, meant that it was very difficult to assess how many people had been affected and what their immediate needs were – crucial information for the supply chain to be set up and managed effectively.

Despite such forbidding circumstances, the rate at which the relief teams worked and what they were able to achieve in just a few days, with very modest means, was impressive. For example, the IFRC managed to mobilize a global supply chain in a very agile

---

and flexible way. Within 30 days the organization had chartered 45 planes, amassed 255,000 blankets, 34,000 tents, and 120,000 plastic sheets. Within 100 days they had secured the assistance of 300,000 people and €23 million. Impressive, given that they started from scratch with virtually no money. Also while they were mobilizing resources for Gujarat, they were still involved in other disasters such as the earthquake in El Salvador, drought in Tajikistan, volcanic activity at Mt Merapi, Indonesia, and the Orissa cyclone in India.

The fruits of its work earned the IFRC public recognition and allowed it to be accepted by other organizations arriving after it as the natural leader. However, the Gujarat relief operation was not without its problems. Adequate feedback and greater reflection served to highlight where it still had room for improvement.

FIVE KEY BUILDING BLOCKS OF PREPAREDNESS

Preparedness (à la IFRC) consists of five key building blocks that have to be in place to produce effective results. They deal with Human Resources, Knowledge Management, Logistics, Financial Resources, and Community. To be better prepared and therefore respond more effectively all five blocks need to be interconnected (see Figure 3.2).

The systems and departments need to be set up so that they enable the five flows (material, information, finance, people, and knowledge) to be most efficient; for example, the flow of goods from the entry points where there is adequate absorption capacity onto where they are most needed (material flow), information to ensure collaboration and coordination (information flow), and funds from donor support (financial flows).

Human Resources

This comprises well-selected and adequately trained people. A frequent issue for humanitarian organizations is the limited pool of trained staff or experts, and the limited ability to train staff. As we discussed in Chapter 1, the sector is also affected by high staff turnover with a strong reliance on volunteers. In general, the incentives for professionalization are small albeit rising, and thus much of the work is based on devotion and motivation, which is cyclical and hard to channel consistently. As most disasters involve an international staff, HR deals with multicultural issues in their operations that also need to be considered. By focusing on the human resource aspect of preparedness, humanitarian organizations are able to create professional tracks for their best people in order to keep them, and make use of volunteers and secondments in better-defined situations.

Knowledge Management

In Chapter 6 we discuss how learning from previous disasters (i.e., capturing, codifying, and transferring knowledge about logistics operations) is a critical issue for most organizations that, as mentioned before, suffer from high staff turnover. Given the limited availability of trained staff, most people go from one disaster to another with very little time to document what they learned in each circumstance. The challenge is to build upon those lessons and communicate them across the organization to ensure that tacit knowledge becomes explicit and part of the organizational culture. Management must drive the knowledge-capturing process and set the incentives for people to share and use knowledge. This could be aligned with the professional tracks mentioned earlier by motivating staff to become specialists in one area (e.g., water sanitation or telecommunications), and requiring that others tap into that knowledge to develop a minimum level of competence in every specialty.

Logistics

Appropriate skills in process and logistics management are critical, as logistics earns respect as a central function in the IFRC and other organizations like WFP. Raising operations and process management to such a level at the IFRC required a change in the organizational structure with new divisions; a new strategy (standardizing items and agreements, commodity tracking system, inventory management, etc.); and new logistics functions from procurement all the way down to planning, warehouse management, training, and reporting.

Financial Resources

Sufficient financial resources, rapidly deployable during emergencies (liquidity), and the ability to fundraise during the disaster for the post-disaster and continuous preparedness phases (budget forecasting) are essential elements. The challenge for finance is to broaden the donor base and to remain free of political agendas to guarantee the organization's neutrality above all. Yet it must be flexible enough to allocate as needs change (avoiding earmarked donations). Financing is a competition, very much based on the public's attachment to and recognition of the brand and their perception of the organization's effectiveness. Therefore, visibility is an issue. Internally, finance deals also with the agency's obligations to its upstream and downstream partners (transparency and accountability will be discussed in Chapter 5).

Community

Finding effective ways of collaborating with other key players (governments, military, business, and other humanitarian organizations) that make up the humanitarian ecosystem is increasingly important. In some instances this may mean becoming the "channel captain" for certain issues (or "lead agency," to use UN terminology), but overall it requires being able to work with and tap into the knowledge and expertise of each group rather than duplicating efforts. In Chapter 4 we discuss coordination with different stakeholders in greater detail.

PREPAREDNESS STRATEGY DRIVES RESPONSE EFFECTIVENESS

A strong preparedness strategy based on the five building blocks (Human Resources, Knowledge Management, Logistics, Financial Resources, and Community) allows for the development of a Triple-A humanitarian supply chain (see Chapter 1). In turn the Triple-A supply chain facilitates an effective response without excessive firefighting (see Figure 3.3).

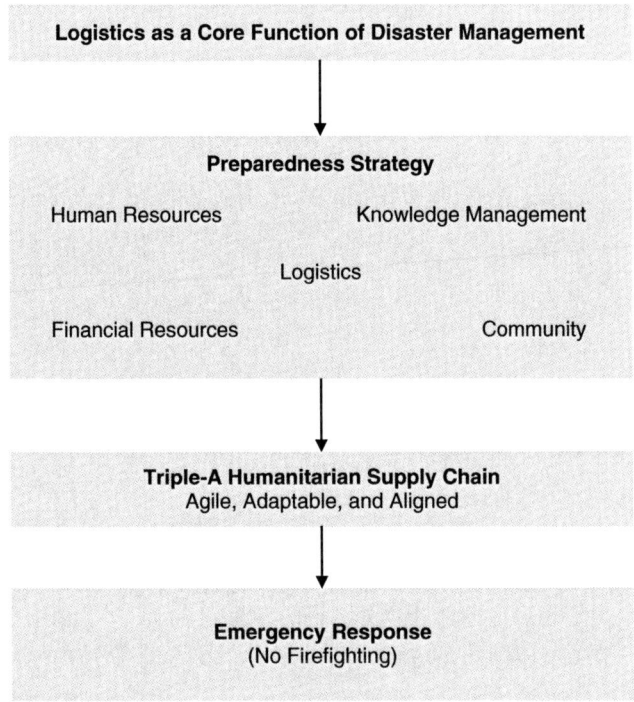

FIGURE 3.3 **Preparedness Strategy Drives Response Effectiveness**

Table 3.2 illustrates how the five building blocks of preparedness strategy drove the development of a Triple-A supply chain at the IFRC and made it a recognized leader in the humanitarian sector.

PUT AN END TO FIREFIGHTING

We started this chapter by arguing that successful disaster responses are not improvised. Humanitarian organizations still too often find themselves caught unprepared and moving into firefighting mode. Firefighting can be prevented

TABLE 3.2 **Five Building Blocks of Preparedness Drive Triple-A Supply Chain Response at the IFRC**

Elements	Agile	Adaptable	Aligned
Human Resources	• Develop Relief Emergency Response Units at different levels that can be deployed within 12–24 hours of a disaster.	• Continuously train staff at all levels on the experiences gained in different disasters and the latest organizational developments. • Create a dialogue for knowledge exchange between the National Societies and the IFRC.	• Between the IFRC and the National Societies to maintain a pool of experts that the FACT team can draw upon and recruit. • Create incentives for career development, training, and mobility across the National Societies and IFRC.
Knowledge Management	• Process previously captured information so that it is readily available as a reference point for those operating in the field. • Provide contact information of colleagues who have developed specific skills so that they can be easily contacted in cases where advice is needed.	• Codify systematically all lessons learned in the past and disseminate them in modules so that staff can adapt them to the different circumstances they face in the field.	• Collect information on previous operations from people at different levels of the organization (specialist, international and local staff, volunteers). • Provide incentives for sharing information.

Logistics	• The ability to track and trace the flow of goods through a commodity tracking system. • Setting up prepositioned goods and buffer inventories. • Frequently exchanging information about needs with all interested parties.	• Contingency planning and crisis management teams to simulate scenarios and forecast potential changes in design or product. • Flexible products and designs (such as kits).	• Collaborative relationships with their partners with clear definitions of roles and tasks. • Pre-negotiated agreements with suppliers.
Finance	• Putting in place immediate response accounts to activate program. • Avoiding reliance on earmarked funds.	• Develop broader base of donors with more flexible funds that will maintain the operation free of political agendas while allocating funds on the ground as needed.	• Negotiate relationships with credit terms that reflect the funding cycle. • Being transparent and accountable to prove their fund-raising efficiency and brand credibility.
Community	• Tapping into others' expertise and knowledge. • Liaise with local actors to increase ability to forecast and plan.	• Strategic alliances to deploy and tap into specialized or local knowledge, specific to each need.	• Strategic alliances ensuring better access to information and visibility of the actions of the other members in the ecosystem.

using tactical, strategic, or cultural methods,[6] all of which we find embedded in the preparedness strategy discussed above.

Tactical

- Add problem solvers with the relevant skills. This is particularly relevant for areas in which expertise is required like shelter, water sanitation, and telecommunications. It can also apply to areas where more manpower is required (volunteers) for distribution or tracking goods and people.
- Shut down operations. While not necessarily possible all the time, this tactic should definitely be considered in situations when continuing the efforts would worsen the crisis; for example, postponing distribution of aid for a short period until enough goods are available to meet the target group.
- Perform triage and consider that not all problems will get solved, and thus prioritize. This is often seen in operations when agencies prioritize bottlenecks along the way to solve big impact problems first, or when they prioritize who will receive aid when there is not enough for everyone.

Strategic

- Change design strategy, for example in areas with limited or difficult access or where other partners are better equipped to work. This is often seen when two agencies coordinate to distribute aid on the same day to the beneficiaries.
- Outsource to implementing partners and locals with the right capacity and skills. Through joint distribution

NGOs may consolidate some of the tasks, thereby serving more people in a shorter span of time and with fewer resources.

- Cluster problems to solve them in groups in order to maximize impact. Some problems could be outsourced to more capable partners, while other problems may require a combination of skills from different actors.
- Develop problem solvers, by training and reinforcing local capacity. This goes beyond tactical training; it is giving people the ability through clearly defined roles to become fluent in a subject with a larger understanding of how they fit in the overall process. In areas where there are recurring operations, this is a good strategy to adopt in collaboration with the local actors. For instance, locals can be trained to assist in data collection and information gathering (see Chapter 5).

Cultural

- Do not tolerate firefighting and enforce objectives. Even though the situation and the needs in the field are constantly changing, enforce people's job description and provide support so that they perform toward jointly agreed objectives (rather than putting out fires). An example could be assessment teams going to the field and getting involved in the implementation, rather than focusing on providing the information they are expected to supply for the subsequent stages to be implemented.
- Do not push deadlines at all cost and try to understand the changing conditions on the field. As mentioned earlier, in some cases delaying distribution of aid (as long as it does not affect the population) may have greater benefits for all parties.

- Do not reward firefighting and measure performance against the agreed objectives.

CONCLUSION

Too often the needs in the field exceed the organization's capacity to respond, making humanitarian organizations operate constantly from one disaster to another non-stop. At the same time funding for the organizations is for the most part linked to emergency response, leaving little or no resources to build up capacity between disasters. As a result of the fast pace and the limited resources, preparedness can easily be overlooked.

However, numerous (and recurring) examples show that preparedness does pay off, and that despite the ability of humanitarian organizations to respond with limited information and resources, a well-prepared response is much more effective. Based on the tasks and skills required to respond we argued that supply chain management should be at the center of the preparedness strategy of any organization to enhance the flow of material, information, finance, people, and knowledge. These flows will be supported by the organization's Human Resources, Knowledge Management, Logistics, Financial Resources, as well as its Community relations (five building blocks of preparedness). The ultimate goals of these departments will be to ensure that the execution rolls out a Triple-A supply chain that is aligned, agile, and adaptable, for which there is little to no firefighting.

4

COORDINATION

INTRODUCTION

In Chapter 1 we emphasized the importance of careful design and good coordination to ensure the efficient functioning of the supply chain and its different components. Here, we discuss in detail the need for coordination between humanitarian organizations, and the levels and means through which coordination happens. We also discuss the challenges of coordinating during an emergency.

While coordination with the military is beyond the scope of this book, the important thing to consider is the issue of neutrality in protecting the humanitarian space, especially in conflict zones. The nature of military intervention is political, which is not compatible with the humanitarian mandate. However, there are clear areas where collaboration is allowed as recommended and prescribed in the Oslo Agreement and the IASC Working Paper from 24 June 2004.[1]

Coordination with the media is also important and we will touch on that later in Chapter 5 on information management. Coordination with the private sector will be dealt with in detail in Chapter 7, addressing Corporate Social Responsibility (CSR) and cross-learning for the private sector.

THE NEED FOR COORDINATION

Even though the humanitarian ecosystem is certainly not restricted to the UN and its agencies, many field workers would claim informally that it is not until the UN arrives in a country or region that the gates truly open for aid to flow. Other humanitarian agencies can, and do, go into countries or regions on their own before the UN arrives, but often they lack the political support and recognition of the UN system. For that reason, let us start by examining coordination from the UN's perspective.

When the UN humanitarian system was designed, several decades ago, agencies and programs were divided into specialized mandates (e.g., WFP for food, UNHCR for refugees, UNICEF for children, WHO for health). However, no crisis is ever just about children, or food, or health alone. This highlights the fact that these agencies must work together to achieve sustainable and comprehensive results. Likewise, the majority of the UN programs are actually implemented through NGO partners with the support and blessing of the local communities and governments, so these other stakeholders need to be included in the coordination game.

At their creation, the UN agencies lacked an effective mechanism to foster inter-agency dialogue or help coordinate operations, let alone a mechanism that could break down the silos that existed in field operations. Coordination, as such, became an orphan issue in the humanitarian system, leading to substantial inefficiencies, including the wasteful duplication of efforts.

Coordination is not meant to be another layer of bureaucracy or an additional step in the humanitarian system. So the idea has never been to create another independent organization to be a coordinator. Instead, the correct notion is to create a platform for coordination where the agencies can interact and exchange their concerns – and assets. Along that idea this chapter explains the work of the UN Office for the Coordination of Humanitarian Affairs (OCHA) and the United Nations Joint Logistics Center (UNJLC) (see Boxes 4.1[2] and 4.2[3]).

Box 4.1: A Brief History of OCHA

In December 1991, the General Assembly adopted Resolution 46/182, designed to strengthen the UN's response to both complex emergencies and natural disasters. In addition, it aimed to improve the overall effectiveness of the UN's humanitarian operations in the field.

The resolution also created the high-level position of Emergency Relief Coordinator (ERC). This new function would combine into a single UN focal point the functions carried out by representatives of the Secretary General for major and complex emergencies, as well as the UN natural disaster functions carried out by the UN Disaster Relief Organizations (UNDRO) Coordinator.

Soon after, the Secretary General established the Department of Humanitarian Affairs (DHA) and assigned the ERC the status of Under Secretary General (USG) for Humanitarian Affairs, with offices in New York and Geneva to provide institutional support.

Resolution 46/182 also created the Inter-Agency Standing Committee (IASC), the Consolidated Appeals

---

Box 4.1: (Continued)

Process (CAP), and the Central Emergency Revolving Fund (CERF) as key coordination mechanisms and tools of the ERC.

As part of the Secretary General's program of reform in 1998, DHA was reorganized into the Office for the Coordination of Humanitarian Affairs or OCHA. Its mandate was expanded to include the coordination of humanitarian response, policy development, and humanitarian advocacy.

The Office for the Coordination of Humanitarian Affairs carries out its coordination function primarily through the IASC, which is chaired by the ERC. Participants include all humanitarian partners, from UN agencies, funds, and programs to the Red Cross Movement and NGOs. The IASC ensures inter-agency decision-making in response to complex emergencies. These responses include needs assessments, consolidated appeals, field coordination arrangements, and the development of humanitarian policies.

Budget and Staffing

The core functions of OCHA are supported by approximately 860 staff members in New York, Geneva, and in the field. OCHA's budget for 2006 was US$128 million, of which about 10 percent comes from the regular UN budget and the remainder from extra-budgetary sources donated by member states and donor organizations.

Emergency Relief Coordinator

The functions of the ERC are focused on three core areas: (a) policy development and coordination functions in support of the Secretary General, ensuring that all humanitarian issues, including those which fall between gaps in existing mandates of agencies such as protection and assistance for internally displaced persons, are addressed; (b) advocacy of humanitarian issues with political organs, notably the Security Council; and (c) coordination of humanitarian emergency response, by ensuring that an appropriate response mechanism is established, through IASC consultations, on the ground.

Box 4.2: UNJLC Activation

The UNJLC is activated through an inter-agency consultation among decision-makers designated by the Inter-Agency Standing Committee Working Group (IASC-WG). The IASC is the primary mechanism for inter-agency coordination of humanitarian assistance. The IASC-WG is composed of the directors of the Emergency Programs of the IASC agencies or their equivalent counterparts. It is a unique forum involving the key UN and non-UN humanitarian partners.

A decision to activate the UNJLC is made within 24 hours on the basis of the scale of the crisis, existing agency capabilities, the extent of bottlenecks, possible use of MCDA (Military/Civil Defense Assets), and situation assessments by the UNJLC Unit.

Box 4.2: (Continued)

Once the decision to activate has been taken deployment takes place within 48 hours. In the case of complex emergencies involving a peacekeeping or multinational military force, activation will be coordinated with the relevant authorities. In this case, the Special Representative of the Secretary General (SRSG) and/or the UN Resident/Humanitarian coordinator should be consulted.

In sudden-onset disasters, the consultation process will take place in close coordination with the relevant UN-designated official, OCHA, and the Local Emergency Management Authority (LEMA). The UNJLC may be represented on UNDAC[4] missions to assess inter-agency logistics coordination structures and requirements.

The OCHA has a broad mandate to cover all issues related to humanitarianism. Logistics is just another issue with no particular ranking or priority (depending on the nature of the crisis). However, logistics requires significant attention to forecast and prevent bottlenecks, coordinate efficient flow of goods, and monitor response to needs. For logistical matters, OCHA has increasingly relied on the UNJLC wherever they both operate.

UNJLC Logistics Coordination Platform

The UNJLC is given the mandate to coordinate and optimize the logistics capabilities of humanitarian organizations in large-scale emergencies. The UNJLC operates under the custodianship of the WFP, which is responsible for the administrative and financial management of the center, and it is funded by voluntary contributions channeled through WFP (see Boxes 4.2 and 4.3).

Box 4.3: The UNJLC: The Afghanistan Crisis

The United Nations Joint Logistics Center operations in the Afghanistan crisis were started in late September 2001 out of World Food Program offices in Rome. As all international staff had been evacuated from Afghanistan because of the hostilities in early October 2001, a UNJLC was established in Islamabad, Pakistan. The UNJLC Rome was to coordinate strategic logistics planning issues (i.e., movement of supplies into the crisis region), while the UNJLC Islamabad would concentrate on the regional logistics issues (i.e., movement of goods from the region into Afghanistan). Overall, the UNJLC was responsible for logistics coordination and not actual management of logistics assets such as warehouses, trucks, or aircrafts. These activities were the responsibility of each individual agency.

As it had no cargo of its own to move, the UNJLC established a neutral, regular forum to discuss logistics issues and task resources, and to set priorities. To help agencies reduce cost and volume and maximize the use of limited resources they focused on airlifts. In practice, they compiled the inventory of available assets (military aircraft and planes chartered by UN agencies or provided by donors), capacity, and agency requirements. Taking into account humanitarian priorities, they assigned assets to agencies or advised them on pooling of assets for long-range airlifts. Their

---

Box 4.3: (Continued)

purpose was not to interfere with the humanitarian agencies' well-established chartering agreements. Instead, they coordinated the capacity to achieve synergies and efficiency. Keep in mind that it was common practice for agencies to charter airplanes separately, without coordinating with each other.

The UNJLC aimed to ensure that excess aircraft capacity was efficiently used, for example, if an agency could not justify chartering an entire aircraft for a small load. Their objective was to match eventual overcapacity with outstanding transport requests. To perform satisfactorily, the UNJLC required timely and accurate information, and inputs from each agency in terms of their assets. This way the UNJLC became informally the repository of information regarding agency strategic airlifts into the region.

The general consensus was that the humanitarian community obtained significant benefits by coordinating. While there is no quantitative evidence to assess the magnitude of the cost reduction, it is clear that in this case the humanitarian community benefited from consolidating their purchasing power to obtain better deals with their service providers, maximizing the use of space in aircraft, keeping their inventory low, improving their planning and forecasting throughout the supply chain, minimizing competition for resources among partners, increasing their service level since the UNJLC prioritized cargo based on beneficiary needs.

In the initial stages of most operations the UNJLC focuses on dispersing bottlenecks in logistics by opening transport corridors and border crossing points. The UNJLC also focuses on deconflicting the use of common logistics assets such as airspace and airfields with military forces. The UNJLC's responsibilities are usually defined on a case-by-case basis but generally include the following:[5]

- Logistics support at operational planning, coordination, and monitoring level. Unless otherwise specified, UN agencies and other humanitarian bodies established in the area continue to exercise their normal responsibilities. As a result, the UNJLC will not be involved in policy-making or establishing humanitarian needs and priorities.
- Collecting, analyzing, and disseminating logistics information relevant to the ongoing humanitarian operation.
- Monitoring the movement of humanitarian cargo and relief workers within the crisis area, using commonly available transport assets.
- Managing the import, receipt, dispatch, and tracking of food and non-food relief commodities that have not been assigned to an agency.
- Writing assessments of roads, bridges, airports, ports, and other logistics infrastructure, and recommending actions for repair and reconstruction.
- Serving as an information platform for supporting humanitarian logistics operations and for recommending the most efficient modes of transportation.
- Coordinating the use of available warehouse capacity.
- Coordinating the influx of strategic humanitarian airlift into the crisis area.

- Identifying logistical bottlenecks and proposing satisfactory solutions or alternatives.
- Facilitating measures with local authorities for importing, transporting, and distributing relief commodities into the country.
- Providing reliable information regarding the logistics capacity for meeting targets (see Box 4.3[6]).

LEVELS OF COORDINATION

As discussed in previous chapters, humanitarian operations take shape at different levels. The same holds true for coordination, and it can take place at three levels:

- *International Level*: This includes the UN Security Council, national governments, headquarters of the participating agencies, and their respective donors.
- *National Level*: This includes local authorities, military, civil society, and the local representatives of the agencies and NGOs.
- *Field Level*: This includes humanitarian field staff, and beneficiaries.

International Level

At this level, coordination is subject to the whims and demands of the political establishment. National governments, aware of their limitations, invite and open the door to international aid agencies to support the relief efforts, as did Indonesia during the Indian Ocean tsunami.

Part of the tsunami response process included the activation of the UNJLC by the IASC with specific tasks and objectives. Few examples are listed below:

- Air Coordination Cell for Strategic and Regional Air Operations: Prioritize requirements for air transportation; liaise with regional and local air management entities; and provide timely and accurate information on air transport operations.
- Movement Coordination: Assist in establishing surface and air corridors and deconflict with military entities; through a Movement Coordination Center assist with movement control of cargo and people.
- General Logistics Coordination: Establish and support appropriate inter-agency logistics coordination structures at all levels of the operation; through this process, identify and address any logistics bottlenecks affecting the humanitarian efforts as a whole.

At the international level countries also discuss the priorities for the international aid and development agenda at the UN Security Council, or even put pressure on certain nations failing to address the needs of their population or committing genocide.

National Level

At this level, the most important challenge is to have all stakeholders agree that coordination is necessary for the success of the operation and to commit to making it work. For example, the national authorities need to welcome the acts of solidarity from the international community into their country. Foreign aid cannot be imposed and needs to abide by the conditions of the national authorities. Then the Humanitarian Resident Coordinator needs to work with all the different humanitarian agencies present in the country to liaise with the national authorities and harmonize the response. At time, he/she may be required to negotiate access or support from the national authorities to support the humanitarians. There is also a need to oversee the performance of the aid to make sure, as we discussed earlier, that it is neutral and impartial according to the principles.

Accepting the need for coordination is an issue best addressed in the preparation stage. Iraq is one of the few examples where coordination was accepted ahead of time during the preparation phase. The anticipation of the events in Iraq gave the humanitarian community time to develop a contingency plan and define the operational roles upon activation in Iraq, including the assignment of coordinators.

Field Level

At this level, coordination is a function of personal interaction and leadership. It is based on how well the coordinator understands the local needs and context, and how well he/she is recognized by his/her peers as a leader. The key to a successful implementation rests upon understanding what are the local needs and coping mechanisms. For example, during the 2006 Israeli–Lebanese conflict the humanitarian aid workers on the ground quickly took advantage of the spontaneous support of the Lebanese community for its fellows. This support substantially reduced the amount of goods that needed to be imported and allowed the aid agencies to focus more on the reinstitution of security.

In moments of pressure it is important to work with people who are recognized as knowledgeable and reliable. There is a pool of humanitarian workers that have worked on most major disasters, and by reference build a reputation that at the onset of every disaster makes them credible among their peers (see e.g., Box 4.4).

Box 4.4: Coordinating Air Operations at the Onset of the Indian Ocean Tsunami

On 30 December 2004 just four days after the tsunami, a retired Air Force General was sent to Banda Aceh in Indonesia on behalf of the UNJLC.

As an officer he was used to traditional military methods of coordination with clear lines of authority and communication, where participation is guaranteed, and funds and resources are readily available for specific goals. As a humanitarian he could rely on none of these factors. As a newcomer to the humanitarian world, he was recruited as air operations specialist in Sudan, but when the tsunami hit, he was diverted to Banda Aceh. The only information coming out of the area at that time was contained in news broadcasts by the likes of CNN and the BBC.

Scarce information was only the tip of the iceberg. There were too many players fighting for limited access to essential resources and assets. Relief agencies were actually competing and wildly duplicating efforts. There were no effective or reliable telecommunications linking headquarters, regional offices, or

---

Box 4.4: (Continued)

incoming flights. Basically, the former General had no means to predict what support might be sent from his colleagues at the regional office or what types of donations were in the relief pipeline. Besides this lack of any communication infrastructure, the local airfield was small and insufficient for the magnitude of needs. There were no storage facilities and no forklifts or handling equipment to work with. There was a shortage of local skills and no time to train them.

Security was still a concern in an area that had experienced long periods of fighting. The weather was not helping either. Rain was incessant, making the ground muddy, reducing visibility, and damaging the goods left out in the open for lack of storage facilities (medicine spoiled, rice fermented, etc.).

The former General's mission was to set up and run the Air Operation Coordination Cell for the humanitarian community. But how could he establish himself as a coordinator? How would he sell the coordination concept? And how would he implement it? In many ways his situation illustrates the main coordination obstacles to humanitarian emergency operations.

As a coordinator, like anyone else, he had to establish and maintain his position in the ecosystem. "You don't just get off the plane and become a coordinator," recalls the former General, "The title alone doesn't make you one or confer operating power." So what does?

The following are the basic skills for any coordinator to establish and sustain their role:

- Contributing new solutions to problems involving multiple parties by motivating them to exchange information or assets.
- Reducing interests of individual parties by trading assets and reducing waste (increasing efficiency).
- Being identified as the coordinator (de facto/de jure leadership) to intervene in matters that concern multiple parties.
- Reinforcing adherence to preset rules to guarantee consistent (or predictable) behavior.
- Building knowledge by creating an understanding of the different factors affecting the operation; most importantly, communicating this knowledge efficiently.

The former General's approach to coordination proved to be effective in that even though the demands of the operation had a strong capacity to overwhelm the capabilities present, he managed to operate in a way that the resources available could be consolidated to prevent the relief effort from becoming a disaster. At the beginning, he acknowledged the intensity of the situation and triaged critical issues focusing on communications as a first priority. He did so by creating periodical reports and looking for ways to set up air communications systems for the airplanes.

DISASTER LIFE CYCLE

Every crisis has a life cycle. As shown in Figure 4.1, one can distinguish three main stages in this cycle: ramp up, sustain, and ramp down (Task Intensity). Each stage demands a different type of coordination based on the objectives and stakeholders involved (Coordination Intensity).

Ramp Up

In the ramp-up stage, time is critical and there is a pressing need to remove the bottlenecks so that the humanitarian community can get to the scene of the disaster quickly. The greater the impact of these bottlenecks, and the larger the number of agencies affected, the closer the problems are to becoming chronic bottlenecks (i.e., those that are

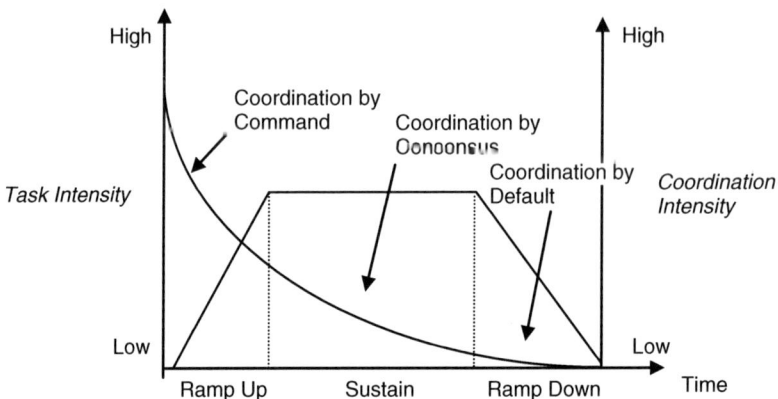

FIGURE 4.1 **Coordination Life Cycle**

Source: The concept of coordination by command, consensus, and default is borrowed from Donini, Antonio. "The Policies of Mercy: UN coordination in Afghanistan, Mozambique, and Rwanda." Occasional Paper #22. Watson Institute for International studies, 1996.

persistent) and the easier the justification for resolution of the problem by an outside coordinator. This is where coordination by command, with its primary benefit of speed of execution, can be very effective. Coordination by command describes a centralized approach where one coordinator pulls together the resources, tasks, and information and generates a solution that is implemented by individual agencies. It requires agreement on responsibilities and objectives, and common territorial areas of responsibility. Simple issues such as obtaining visas, negotiating landing rights, getting customs clearance, arranging licenses for vehicles, signing agreements with the military on accessible corridors and times can all hinder delivery of aid in the initial stages. There is no point in every NGO negotiating with, for example, the Uzbek Government to obtain visas and customs clearance to bring people and goods into Afghanistan. In this case, one organization should take the lead and resolve the issues for all involved (for another example refer to Box 4.4[7]).

Sustain

This stage of the intervention describes a consensus environment that requires individual agencies to sign off on acceptable coordination solutions. Coordination by consensus is when organizations have access to compatible or shared communications equipment, liaison and inter-agency meetings, and pre-mission assessments. For example, as the bottlenecks are cleared and all humanitarian organizations are operational, their focus will shift to fulfilling their own specific mandate (e.g., foodstuffs, health, and water), and ensuring a sustained operation. They no longer accept coordination by command, but may still need some level of coordination. Take for instance fuel which is outside the mandate of any one organization. In Iraq the UNJLC led a study to monitor the use of fuel for humanitarian fleet to predict any shortages before they happened, and ensure that enough fuel was made available in time with priority to those with highest needs.

Ramp Down

The third and final approach, also described as "light coordination" because of its hands-off nature, involves only the collection and dissemination of information through frequent contact between the different actors. In the ramp-down phase, when each individual agency is focused on managing the handover and exit, coordination will still happen but only occasionally and, in a sense, by default. It tends to happen naturally in the field as humanitarians from one organization swap ideas, help, and advice with those from other organizations.

MATCHING THE LIFE CYCLE

Matching the correct type of coordination to the right stage in the life cycle will enable agencies to

- Allocate resources such as money and skilled professionals. The latter is particularly important because the skills needed differ depending on the stage of the life cycle.
- Identify the coordination objectives for each stage and define the performance measurements to be used. Coordination objectives change from one stage to another depending on the intensity of the task; for example, how

should coordinators be evaluated as intensity diminishes through the life cycle? Measurements could include how well they maintain the status quo or how effective they were in implementing the exit strategy.

- Decide on the extent of their involvement. Different teams of skilled specialists are needed at different stages of the disaster.
- Adopt the most efficient approach to implement and monitor the coordination style. For example, some people are able to analyze situations quickly and persuade others to cooperate with new solutions; others may be better at implementing procedures; or perhaps they are good at drawing operations to a close.

Failing to match the right coordination style to the right stage can lead to wasting a lot of resources on wrong goals. Table 4.1 shows some consequences of mismatches in the life cycle.

TABLE 4.1 **Mismatches in the Coordination Life Cycle**

	Ramp Up	**Sustain**	**Ramp Down**
Command	**Match**	• Demands too much control over agencies. • Not focused on strategic issues, maybe too close to execution.	• Mission creep. • Creating dependency inhibiting sustainability and accountability.
Consensus	• Waste of time seeking agreement. • Risk creating early factions.	**Match**	• Insufficient delegation. • Too much involvement in decisions.

TABLE 4.1 **(Continued)**

	Ramp Up	**Sustain**	**Ramp Down**
Default	• Roles are undefined. • Suboptimal use of resources and duplication.	• Roles still unclear. • No central point to monitor performance.	**Match**

HUMANITARIAN COORDINATION: OBSTACLES TO OVERCOME

There are several factors affecting coordination in emergencies linked to the very nature of the environment and the stakeholders involved.

Diversity of Structures

Humanitarian agencies differ greatly in their management structures, cultures, and approach. UN agencies and NGOs lack a harmonized structure making inter-agency communication, decision-making, and basic coordination tricky, to say the least.

Funding

Limited resources breed competition. Agencies also differ in their funding mechanisms which have a direct impact on their flexibility. Earmarked donations pose a challenge for coordination, limiting the ability of agencies on the ground to reallocate resources as they deem most suitable. Donors are increasingly considering inter-agency coordination as a key performance indicator, but the current efforts are only initial steps. Historically, donors have not promoted clear incentives for agencies to collaborate and coordinate. Instead, they have indirectly promoted competition by funding individual agencies based on their stand-alone performance (in addition to earmarked donations), capacity, and, to some extent, branding. In addition, the media places high pressure on the agencies to compete for air time.

Cost

As Minear[8] highlights, coordination is an expensive game for both coordinators and those being coordinated. The direct costs are many: salaries, travel costs to the field for those coordinating, time and money for traveling to meetings for those being coordinated. The indirect costs such as preparing reports and the salaries for those involved in doing this can have a significant financial impact and necessitate a good deal of funding from donors. The time-consuming review processes for joint reports, which are likely to be longer the more agencies are involved, cannot be taken lightly. So given the investment on all sides, the cost/benefit ratio is vitally important for all concerned. If those involved cannot reap additional benefits from the coordinated efforts compared to what they could have achieved in going it alone, then the investment in time and money will have been a waste. On the flip side, if an operation is well coordinated the savings can be substantial as donors have to fund only a central platform instead of administrative costs for various agencies acting alone.

Branding

Perception of the brand is another potential hurdle for coordination. The association of an agency's brand with another has repercussions which the agencies must manage. Agencies need to avoid damage to their brand or misconceptions that could compromise their humanitarian space or license to operate in conflict areas. This is not to say that agencies should not differentiate themselves, but rather that they should coordinate where they would otherwise be competing for access to resources. Agencies rely heavily on a broad base of funding for operational independence, and are reluctant to be associated with certain funding sources. In conflict areas, visibility or donor association is critical to reinforce the agency's neutrality. Eventually, this influences the degree to which agencies work together under the public eye. For example, some agencies refuse assistance from parties involved in the conflict such as the US government in Afghanistan or Iraq.

Leadership

Leadership is perhaps the most important factor in overcoming resistance to coordination. The arguments of cost savings and efficiency alone may not be sufficient. There is a need to have a person with strong leadership qualities who has the political and financial support to engage the different actors in the field. This person should be able to foster collaboration among the different actors.

CONCLUSION

Successful emergency coordination is a mix of different styles (command, consensus, default) for the different stages (ramp up, sustain, and ramp down) of the disaster life cycle, and needs to happen at different levels (international, national, and field).

Coordination is an effort that demands buy-in of all involved and is quintessential in a sector where actors do not have an explicit mandate or reason to be coordinated. In the private sector, companies are driven to coordinate their actions to protect their revenues or profit margins, whereas in the humanitarian sector such clear and easily measurable drivers do not exist. Resistance and obstacles may come from the lack of funding (coordination can be expensive), lack of time, leadership, concerns of visibility and/or incompatible organizational structures or ideologies.

In the humanitarian sector, coordination is even more interesting given the lack of command and control structures known to the private sector and military. Hence the need to exercise top leadership skills supported by information and knowledge management. In Chapters 5 and 6, we will discuss how the latter two are dealt with during emergencies.

5

INFORMATION MANAGEMENT*

INTRODUCTION

On 13 January 2001, the first of two devastating earthquakes struck El Salvador with a magnitude of 7.6 on the Richter scale. Exactly one month, and at least two thousand aftershocks, later, a second earthquake of 6.6 on the Richter scale struck. Combined, the earthquakes caused the deaths of more than a thousand people and injured at least eight thousand more. They also left more than 1 million people homeless (about a sixth of the population) in a country with the highest population density in the world. Economic losses were put at an estimated US$1.6 billion.

For those organizing the immediate response, one of the biggest challenges was getting information (assessment) about the situation on the ground. They needed to know what was affected, what was needed, what resources were available, and, as the aid began to arrive spontaneously, what was coming and when.

---

0 * This chapter quotes extensively from Tomasini, Rolando and Luk Van Wassenhove. "Coordinating Disaster Logistics in El Salvador Using Humanitarian Supply Management System (SUMA)." INSEAD Case Study No.10/2003-5145; and Tomasini, Rolando and Luk Van Wassenhove. "De-politicization of Humanitarian Supply Chain by Creating Accountability: PAHO's Humanitarian Supply Management System." *Journal of International Public Procurement*. Volume 4, Number 3, 2004.

In this chapter we discuss information management as a function that assists in developing visibility, transparency, and accountability. We will link these three aspects of information to the important questions of efficiency and effectiveness as well as discuss how they can help to decouple politics from relief operations.

ROLE OF INFORMATION MANAGEMENT

Information is the foundation upon which the humanitarian supply chain is designed, formed, and managed. As soon as an event like the El Salvador earthquakes takes place, information travels to various sources alerting them to the need for assistance (trigger event). Then the next wave of information will determine demand based on the needs on the ground, and who should participate to meet that demand. Then another wave of information will flow to indicate what has been sent (supply side). Finally, yet another wave will inform how the goods received are being used or meeting the needs, and the cycle repeats itself from the beginning, updating the status of needs.

In Chapter 1, we discussed the different flows that make up a supply chain (Materials, Information, Finance, People, and Knowledge). Information flow needs to be managed like the other flows as a critical component of the supply chain. In the case of many complex emergencies, the UNJLC assumes, to some extent, the role of an information manager. For the purposes of this chapter we adopt their definition of Information Management to build our discussion. This definition was drafted by the organization in the process of defining the mission for their website (www.unjlc.org).

According to UNJLC, Information Management is

1. A space where the humanitarian community can access information resources to provide it with sufficient information to make informed decisions about their work.
2. A provider of information products and services that enable the humanitarian community to do logistics more effectively and efficiently.
3. A focal point for data collection, analysis, and dissemination in support of humanitarian logistics, developing and supporting data standards.
4. An advocate for a culture of information sharing in the humanitarian community, generating awareness of good practice and making it possible for agencies to develop common standards and practices in the field.
5. A basis for the development of a common platform for information-sharing initiatives in the field.

Throughout this chapter we would like to focus on three aspects of information relevant to the humanitarian supply chain: visibility, transparency, and accountability. These should be developed through the information management process.

VISIBILITY (PIPELINE)

Visibility provides a snapshot of what is in the pipeline. It helps determine what resources are missing to improve the response. When the information is compared to the needs (processed), one can identify if the supply chain is doing the right thing (meeting needs) and thus measure its effectiveness.

For example, in the case of El Salvador, the generous response of the international community in support of the affected population was felt immediately. On the day of the first earthquake, 19 airplanes from neighboring countries had already arrived at Comalapa Airport in San Salvador. Considering the magnitude and impact of the damages and the quantity of aid that usually follows, the risk of overwhelming the local logistical capacity was high. This makes it even more critical that the aid provided match the needs to make the best use of limited ground resources such as warehouses, transportation, and trained staff.

El Salvador is a disaster-prone region and thus SUMA was not a new concept to the country. SUMA, Humanitarian Supply Chain Management System/Tracking Methodology, was established by FUNDESUMA[1] and the Pan-American Health Organization (PAHO)[2] to register and track donations coming into a disaster area (see Figure 5.1). The system was used from day one, and achieved full operational capacity within two days. The national emergency response authorities (Comité de Emergencia Nacional, COEN) and other NGOs' public sector stakeholders had been trained previously as part of PAHO's Disaster Reduction and Prevention Program in Latin America. On 14 January 2001, a day after the first earthquake, a Pan-American team of 16 SUMA experts arrived to deploy the full operation, assisted by the Comalapa Airport Fire Brigade. They immediately set up the different units and trained local volunteers, military, and emergency relief personnel to create a self-sustaining local team.

SUMA's presence helped to expedite the flow of goods to recipients. The methodology that supported the software helps to label, prioritize, store, and distribute goods in a very timely and resource-efficient manner. On average, the

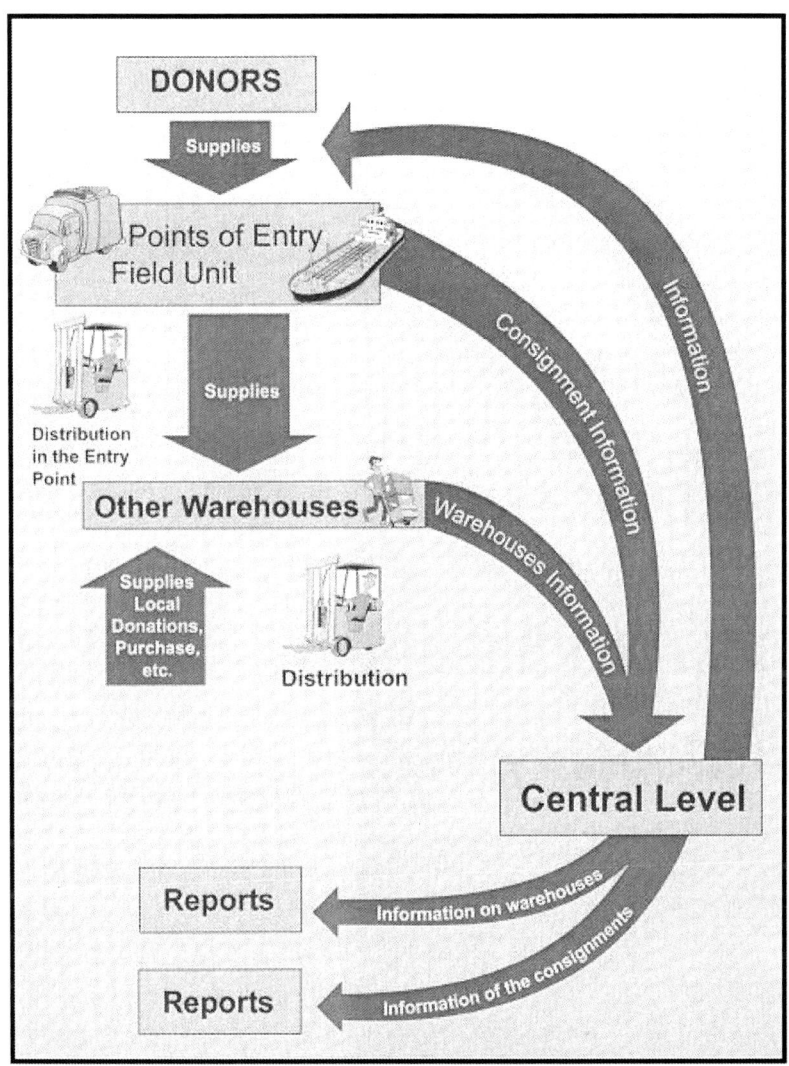

FIGURE 5.1 **SUMA Methodology**
Source: Fundesuma.

goods were processed within 12 hours from reception to distribution. At the same time, SUMA produced comprehensive periodic reports that gave snapshots of the needs and status of donations. Having a standardized systematic approach with an intuitive and user-friendly interface made it easier to rotate the human capital that so rigorously devoted endless hours over consecutive days, without losing momentum.

By the end of March 2001, SUMA had registered 16,000 tons of goods arriving in approximately 900 flights from 41 countries. While all of this assistance was extremely helpful to the population, if the local authorities had not been ready to receive it, imagine the logistical bottlenecks and conflicts this could have created.

TRANSPARENCY (PROCESS)

While visibility provides information about the content in the pipeline, transparency provides an insight into the processes. For example, one may be aware that 10 tons of wheat are on their way to the warehouse (visibility), but not certain if they are being delivered by the quickest or cheapest route.

We define transparency as the ability to understand how processes interact within the supply chain to improve performance. As such, transparency helps to answer the question of efficiency: are we doing it well? The answer will enable agencies to redesign steps in the process, determine procurement needs, or help donors allocate their funds.

Building on the El Salvador example, consider how goods were sourced during the crisis. A large percentage came from donations (in kind) to meet the highest priority needs.

The rest came from procurement, which was financed with funds donated by individuals and governments. However, the challenging question was what to buy. To answer that, humanitarians needed to identify gaps in donations which can be done only when there is sufficient visibility.

Procurement tends to be a very effective way to meet specific needs with accuracy and speed. Wherever possible, the purchases are made locally to stimulate the economy and minimize costs, or through preferential agreements with international suppliers.

In El Salvador, the National Committee for Solidarity (Comité Nacional de Solidaridad, CONASOL), a private sector committee, was created by President Francisco Flores to manage the collection of donated funds, and procurement and distribution processes of relief efforts. Reports indicate that 56 percent of the goods registered by SUMA were purchased by CONASOL using cash donations.

Under the watchful eye of the international community and humanitarian stakeholders, CONASOL had the challenging task of procuring the right amount of goods, at the right time, to be delivered to the right place. They relied on the reports from SUMA to track the activities taking place in the humanitarian supply chain (incoming goods, goods in transit, stored, distributed, or unsolicited).

The procurement process is judged not only by how well the funds are managed but also by the quality of the response. In a humanitarian operation, this translates into speed and accuracy. For these two characteristics, SUMA was judged by the users to be valuable in harmonizing the procurement process with operational standards that expedited reception and distribution of goods. SUMA's methodology set out guidelines for packaging and labeling, for categorization of goods, and prioritization. The harmonization of these processes enabled goods to be rapidly available for distribution at the airport reception point without creating bureaucratic bottlenecks or confusion. Accuracy depended on how well CONASOL assessed the needs, and this included using SUMA's report to identify gaps of unmet needs in the supply chain and allocating funds for their procurement.

As with any financial process, CONASOL had to ensure that all their transactions were transparent and acceptable to public scrutiny. Procurement demands a great deal of transparency to make sure that there is no manipulation or diversion of funds. Therefore, having a tracking system that could quickly generate reports with clear and objective data was extremely helpful to clarify any confusion and prevent rumors of mismanagement. In particular, SUMA helped to show how funds were allocated. It showed when and where the goods were received, and how they were distributed.

ACCOUNTABILITY (PARTIES/PERFORMANCE)

Accountability identifies who is responsible for the actions within the process and how well they are performed. Having identified that 10 tons of rice are to be shipped to the warehouse and the most efficient route to do so, this is the part where one could identify the best party to do the transport or, if delivery is unsuccessful, who failed to do their part in the process.

Accountability is a key issue in such complex environments. As discussed throughout this book, the humanitarian ecosystem is made up of many different groups with different incentives and levels of commitment. There is the public sector, which includes government agencies, the emergency relief system, the military and local authorities. There is the private sector with corporations, service providers, goods suppliers, and individuals. In between, there is the international community and the large and small aid agencies. Lastly, there is society at large which, regardless of its condition prior to the disaster, is exposed to unexpected changes after the disaster. Among all these stakeholders there is a plethora of incentives and mandates that need to be coordinated for an effective response. Failure to do so would be at the expense of optimal performance and ultimately the well-being of those in critical need of assistance. To coordinate all these stakeholders, some level of accountability needs to exist, assigning responsibilities, and reporting on the actions of each party.

Accountability Cycle

Accountability as the ultimate outcome of better information management can be achieved through a four-stage cycle that eventually supports the interactivity between stakeholders[3] (see Figure 5.2).

1. *Responsibility*: Assigning who is responsible for which tasks based on assessments.
   The first stage has to do with defining the roles and responsibilities of each stakeholder. In El Salvador this was clear for international aid agencies and donors. On the local front, there was some initial confusion between government agencies (COEN and CONASOL), but that was quickly resolved as each defined its strengths and capabilities. Likewise, responsibility included determining who should run warehouses, who is responsible for

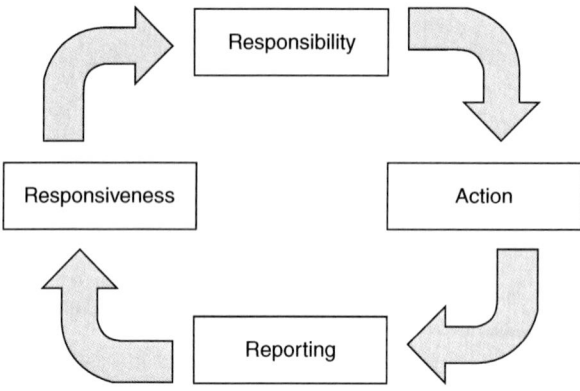

	Accountability	Concept	SUMA
STAGES OF ACCOUNTABILITY CYCLE	Agreement on clear roles and responsibilities	Define roles and Responsibilities.	Government, along with COEN and CONASOL, has main responsibility for management of the humanitarian supply chain.
	Taking action	Stakeholders' ability to execute their roles.	Operations are set up using the SUMA software and units design. SUMA assists personnel in recording incoming goods, managing the warehouse, tracking distribution, and assessing need gaps.
	Reporting	Ability to communicate clearly and objectively.	The system generates objective information on the management of the goods entering and needed in the supply chain. Charts, graphs, and statistics are communicated to all stakeholders including media, communities, and donors.
	Responding	Capacity to empower others to act.	As the information is divulged the needs become apparent and associated stakeholders become automatically responsible.

FIGURE 5.2 **Accountability Cycle**

security, transportation, reporting, and all the related functions of the supply chain.

2. *Taking Action*: Executing your assigned duties.

   The second stage involves the ability of each stakeholder to act on the duties for which they are responsible.

Hopefully this is not a big problem since parties will be assigned the duty they are most qualified to perform. However, in dynamic environments many things can happen and thus it is important that anomalies or changes be communicated immediately.

3. *Reporting*: Making public the actions taken.

   The third stage involves the ability to communicate clear and objective information. This stage, like the previous, was supported by SUMA's capacity to collect and process all the data and to generate reports that supported the humanitarian organizations' decision-making process while informing the public of the organizations' activities.

4. *Responding*: Influencing others to compliment your efforts.

   The fourth stage involves responding to and complying with agreed standards of performance and the views and needs of the stakeholders.

BENEFITS OF ACCOUNTABILITY

Building on the example of El Salvador, where humanitarian aid was deployed in a heavily politicized environment, it is believed that having a tool like SUMA in place, establishing transparency through the use of information, is critical to depoliticizing the ecosystem. What happened in El Salvador was an opportunity to show that trust in the government could be achieved. For that, the transparency and accountability provided by SUMA's methodology was very useful.

At the time of the earthquake, El Salvador was still recovering socially and politically from the scars of a 12-year civil war that took the lives of approximately 75,000 people. The incumbent government faced strong opposition from a significant portion of the population, who identified themselves with the opposition party. A section of the population had doubts about the government's ability and approach to managing the aid.

However, in an independent survey,[4] when asked if SUMA facilitated transparency in the management of assistance to disaster areas, the consensus was positive. In fact, evaluators noted that this question generated the most animated responses from the interview subjects, and SUMA's contribution to transparency was repeatedly emphasized without prompting. In summary, what the results and studies show is that having a system for accountability in place

- Minimizes the likelihood of "conflict connection" and protects humanitarian space by giving snapshots of the operations, enabling stakeholders and managers to judge whether the aid is distributed in accordance with humanitarian principles (see Box 5.1).
- Assists in the division of tasks resulting in a better distribution of labor based on who is most appropriate to perform each job, subsequently reducing duplication of efforts, and suboptimal performance.
- Improves donor relations by helping donors to know when and where their funds or goods were used, and whether they were indeed used for genuine humanitarian purposes.
- Improves media relations by proactively providing reports about the performance of the supply chain, so

that the media can communicate objective and readily available information to the communities in a way that facilitates planning with outside stakeholders (tell people what is needed, what is not needed anymore, how well the aid is distributed, which areas still have pending needs or need extra support, minimize the likelihood of speculations and rumors).

- Creates a set of standards to audit the stakeholders' performance. For example, during an evaluation, one can build indicators to determine transparency, responsiveness, and compliance for each stakeholder's operation. Such was the case in El Salvador, where a public–private commission was set up, including PriceWaterhouseCoopers and KPMG, to audit the reception and distribution of goods as well as the management of funds. This audit used SUMA's indicators as well as humanitarian principles as a benchmark for evaluating stakeholder contribution.

Box 5.1: De-politicizing Humanitarian Space

As with any humanitarian operation, all stakeholders, including government, were judged based on adherence to the humanitarian principles of humanity, impartiality, and neutrality in their decisions and actions (see Chapter 2). Given the strong political and social polarization in El Salvador, there were fears that at some levels these principles could have been compromised for political interests of one party over the other.

Box 5.1: (Continued)

Having a neutral coordination body, like the SUMA team, and a coordination tool, like the SUMA software, in place serves as a "gatekeeper" for the humanitarian space. The system is capable of objectively reporting irregularities while instilling a set of operational standards that adhere to the principles at stake.

SUMA's reporting capabilities enable the media to communicate the transparency of the process. In El Salvador reports were generated periodically, outlining the actions taking place at reception points, airports, warehouses, and purchasing. The reports also detailed the distribution and who was involved at each step. Having this information public made it easier for the stakeholders to clarify and avoid any misunderstandings. It also set the boundaries for potential manipulation or diversion, as it would have been easier than usual to track the parties and goods involved.

INFORMATION FLOWS

Data needs to be gathered and processed in order to yield relevant and reliable information that can subsequently be disseminated (see Figure 5.3). The solid arrows in Figure 5.3 show the most desirable information flow in which the data from the field is processed and reported by the humanitarian agencies, the government, or the NGOs associated with the relief efforts to the press and donors

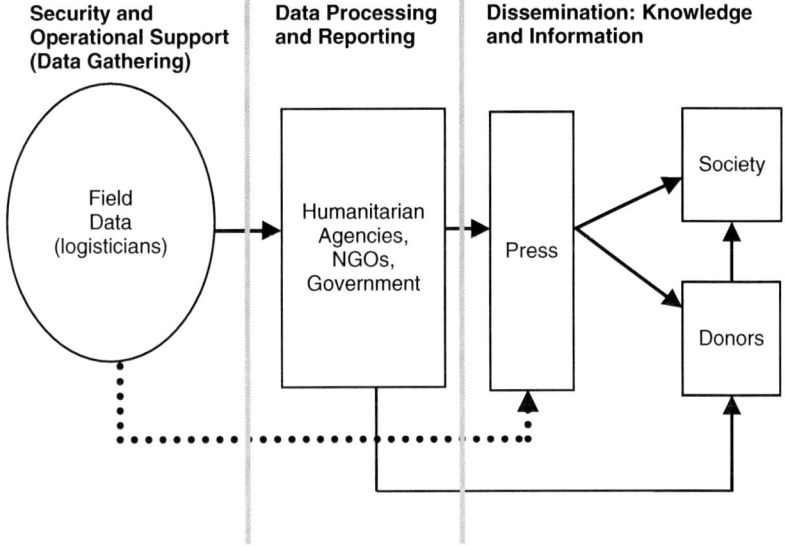

FIGURE 5.3 **Flows and Bottlenecks**

for dissemination in society. When the information travels through the dotted lines, often unofficially, there is a risk of distorting the quality of the information and knowledge management process (knowledge management is discussed in Chapter 6).

Information bottlenecks can be found anywhere from the data gathering to the processing and dissemination processes.

Data Gathering

Talking about their experience as information managers, the UNJLC team says gathering data and information and keeping focus are the main challenges. Former UNJLC Chief Officer Adrian Van der Knaap points out that "If we wait for others to tell us their information needs, we would always be late and add very little value. Instead, we should rely on our team's expertise to identify what is needed and complement what others are missing." The key to a successful process is knowing what data to process at the beginning to disseminate on time to the right audience.

To some extent the main source of information is also the most important recipient – field logisticians. After all, the final information output is developed for them, but they are the ones who gather the raw data to be processed in the first place. Supporting this argument, Douglas Osmond, a former UNJLC Logistics Officer on secondment from the UNHCR, felt that

Logisticians in general need info that is not that tough to get. Most places we go, there are on-going operations so we can recycle information and update it. If you are in the field and have questions you are going to answer them by interacting with colleagues and partners. In most cases, a website is hard to access and decisions need to be made quickly with local and current knowledge.

As such, logisticians are the first source of information (as well as the major target for dissemination).

Humanitarians in the field are in closest contact with needs and they are most knowledgeable about priorities. It is important to find a way of working directly with them to understand what they gather, and help them exchange it equitably. This is necessary to break down barriers of information asymmetry that are so expensive and counter-productive to an operation, and lead to competition and duplication of efforts. What logisticians gather at the beginning is, for the most part, data, unprocessed material such as statistics that can be analyzed to produce actionable information. In general, data is gathered either from the field or from external sources. A network of people collects information by going into communities. They compile readily available data by speaking with locals and observing the situation. For example, staff members in the field would report about fuel prices, exchange rates, security and distances, and transportation costs. All this assumes that there are reliable means of communication for them to share the data with analysts.

External information is easier to obtain provided there are collaboration agreements with the sources. Through partners, the UNJLC website is kept up to date with weather reports, different types of maps, and legal documents, links to other agencies, and information about local services. This information motivates members of the different humanitarian organizations to use the website, since useful information that was otherwise time-consuming to collate on a regular basis now appears.

It is essential that the information providers have a good understanding of the processes involved in the operation, and understand their target audience's needs. Otherwise the opportunity cost of ignoring some piece of information can be very high. At the same time there is not enough capacity to collect and process everything that is available. Prioritization should be based on where the most value is produced.

Sharing data is difficult and yet essential. As with most relationships, parties are not willing or ready to share until they see value. Sometimes parties are unwilling to share because they do not want to assume the cost or invest in the resources needed to share information. Indeed, sharing requires an information manager who makes sure the data represents the facts of the organization, as well as someone writing and answering emails, reading and writing reports, and so on. In light of limited staff and stressful conditions, that could be a critical issue. Frequently, parties see little personal benefit to reporting information that goes to levels in the organization above them only, and that is common knowledge at their level in the field.

Processing

During the gathering process raw data and information are collected to be processed. Data are pieces of fact that need to be interpreted to be useful as information. This is part of the job done at this stage.

However, some of the contributors already share processed data as information. So in this stage of the information management cycle the important thing is to interpret the information and couple it with other pieces for the audience to use it as a decision support package.

To process either data or information, the critical point is to have sufficient capacity to meet the demands on time. Van der Knaap explains that *"In developing information products for emergency operations, you cannot wait months until the final version is ready. You need to focus on the process and be able to provide timely information at each stage, otherwise you are not adding the most value."* The best resource is a pool of knowledgeable and experienced team members who can turn information around quickly into packages that are easily communicated.

The caveat here is that the agencies/NGOs/governments be qualified and credible as institutions to process the data correctly. For example, in heavily politicized environments like El Salvador, the NGO (SUMA) was in a better and more credible position than the government to assume that responsibility. The latter could have fueled further concerns about mismanagement because of its poor historical track record on this subject.

Disseminating

Dissemination is, as Van der Knaap pointed out, perhaps the most challenging part of the information process. He explains, "*We are more likely to succeed if we understand and address our users' needs and habits rather than expecting them to adapt to us. The latter is less likely to happen and would take too much time.*"

The critical points for the dissemination process are audience, accessibility, accuracy of information, and processing timeliness.

Audience

Audience are primarily logisticians in the field, but they are the hardest to satisfy since they are at the same time the ones providing the data. So the value to them of poorly analyzed or delayed information is limited. They are also an audience under pressure; their poor connectivity to the web and their habits in getting information require a different strategy. In Chapter 6 we discuss how information needs to be transformed into knowledge to add the greatest value for decision-making.

Experience shows that most information management services are actually targeted at donors and suppliers upstream in the supply chain. The problem is that unless those providing the information see the benefit of sharing with their upstream partners, the information management process will suffer many limitations (see Box 5.2[5]).

Box 5.2: How the Media and NGOs See the Information Challenge?

A study commissioned by Columbia University, the Fritz Institute, and the Reuters Foundation inter-viewed 54 humanitarian agencies on their relationship with the media. Its conclusions are as follows:

Media

- There is a lack of specialized journalists who can cover most disasters.
- There is a lack of financial resources to attend to each crisis.
- There is a lack of specialist knowledge on humani-tarian issues.
- Short- versus long-term coverage is driven by audi-ence and funding, not needs.
- Audiences are affected by "crisis fatigue" tired of hearing about suffering in regions they cannot relate to.
- There is a feeling that *"Why should my news organi-zation invest in such stories today if they will be there tomorrow and there are so many others that need to be covered today?"*

Humanitarians

- There is a lack of press relations training at field offices.
- There is a lack of donor appreciation for press relations.

- There is a Lack of peer collaboration to jointly address the media.
- *"Journalists are typically interested in bombs, rather than humanitarian issues."*
- *"Journalists are interested in what is going wrong, rather than what is going right."*

Accessibility

Accessibility has to do with the ability to reach the audience through the right vehicles. As discussed earlier, logisticians in the field do not have the time to look up information on the web (see Box 5.3[6]). So what is the right format for this audience? Or better yet, what is a format that would satisfy the broadest audience with minimal investment and highest impact?

There may be better alternatives than text when communicating to a broad audience. Maps not only create a common language but can also be loaded with information about the resources available along the way. Maps can identify in advance information that needs to be regularly updated and invite the users to also become a source for those pieces of information.

Unfortunately, not all questions of accessibility are limited to format. In fact, some are subject to technology and regulations. Technology needs to be available and reliable, as well as user-friendly. It is subject to restrictions imposed by authorities on its use. For example, there are countries in which the government has restrictive policies for communication (lack of freedom of speech). These restrictions can be technological, either because they have strict control over TV or radio channels or because they have censorship over the information that is released by the press. Failure to comply with these regulations can lead to closing down newspapers, shutting down and fining stations, and so on. Unfortunately, some governments still regulate information content and use of technology.

Box 5.3: Technological Challenges of the Development of the UNJLC Website

First Generation: For the first edition of their website in Afghanistan in 2002, the UNJLC hired a local programmer who built a website with off-the-shelf software (Front Page) rather quickly. While useful in making the information public, the format quickly presented accessibility problems. For instance, in the field with a non-Explorer browser, the web links programmed in JavaScript would take a very long time to download and that is assuming the computer had the correct version of Java installed.

Second Generation: A group of consultants had developed a new website image and format, yet the coding was still cumbersome as it was "flat HTML" (see www.unjlc.org). Simplicity and quicker accessibility from the field, where bandwidth and software are often restrictive, became priorities. A new layout and design was launched in March 2003. But even under the new format, simple changes took hours, with new pages or modifications easily taking half a day.

Third Generation: With the operation in Iraq continuing and another starting in Liberia, the website became technically almost unmanageable. The technical demands were too high, and information began to suffer major publication delays. The

---

UNJLC conducted a six-month evaluation of the website, and at this point decided to hire another company to upgrade the website's features. By mid-2004 they launched the third generation of the site with the same domain name and several improvements, as former UNJLC Information Officer Eric Branckaert highlights:

> *The design principles were low bandwidth, consistency in look and feel and standard practices in navigation and the search system. From the user's perspective, the advantage of the new system was that it could send them notifications of updates. For us, the new system gave us an intranet and was much easier to use and update. We could create a new page of information in under a minute and a new sub-crisis area in under a day.*

Although the interface layout remained mostly unchanged, the website assumed a new design and had a new set of features. Considering the different levels of information and communication needs, password-protected intranet and extranet sections were developed. The intranet allowed the UNJLC team members to communicate and share files with a higher level of privacy. Membership at this level included the ability to post or remove files from the other areas of the website.

Accuracy

While the sources may be valid, all types of information have a shelf life, especially in a crisis where everything is dynamic. For example, the UNJLC website is often supplied with information about roads and corridors, but they have to make sure that this is always accurate for logistical planning purposes in environments changing at a fast pace. But even under static conditions parties disseminating information need to confirm the accuracy of what they communicate.

For example, after long periods of conflict, combined with harsh meteorological conditions, Afghanistan's terrain and infrastructure had been drastically affected. The maps that were available did not necessarily reflect the changes that had taken place in the last decade, bringing their accuracy into question. Nigel Snoad, former UNJLC Chief Information Officer, explains,

> *We had to start by making sure that the roads were viable and landmarks still standing. This was not always possible as most of the territory was at highly critical security levels, and there was little infrastructure or time to address the issue. We collaborated with the military to validate the data using their surveillance equipment and made use of the satellite imagery from the Humanitarian Information Centre (HIC) to double check.*

Timeliness

Given that conditions and requirements in a relief operation are constantly changing, the need for information is rapidly evolving. The challenge is to make sure that data is processed as quickly as possible and communicated. This forces humanitarian organizations to prioritize what they will communicate and make sure that they reach their target audience promptly. The latter is a challenge since, as

Osmond points out, *"Logisticians will not have the advantage of accessing a website in the field when trying to make a decision."* Snoad expands, *"Unless you know that people can access the information you are processing quickly before making a decision, you are processing information that will be obsolete and waste your resources."*

Depending on the shelf life of the information, some of it will be processed to support preparedness efforts rather than immediate action. In Chapter 6 (Box 6.1) we discuss the UNJLC's effort to track fuel consumption in Iraq. In addition to giving the website users a regular update on the fuel prices and availability, this helped to predict shortages for the future. This information was useful to plan in advance and avoid disruptions in the humanitarian supply chain due to the lack of fuel.

CONCLUSION

Among the main challenges of an operation are capturing and channeling the wave of information that emerges after the onset of a disaster. Humanitarians struggle to assess the conditions on the ground while trying to raise funds from their donors. Donors try to figure out whom to fund and for what, to have the highest impact on the affected population. Sources of information are for the most part uncoordinated and not always attending to the highest needs. The greatest challenge happens when goods start flying into the area and need to be distributed.

Without proper information it is extremely difficult for humanitarians in the field to prepare for what is coming to the disaster site. As we discussed in this chapter, visibility allows organizations to identify what needs to be appealed, what has been committed, what is in the pipeline, and what is in storage. This information is crucial to ensuring that upon arrival goods will be received and handled properly. Moreover, good information management enables humanitarian organization to build in transparency and communicate what has been distributed (by whom and to whom).

Numerous efforts exist today to harmonize information management in the humanitarian sector with many lessons being transferred from commercial operations. However, technical solutions are only half of the battle, for information exchange is also a behavioral issue.

In the next chapter we will take the concepts of information management even further to discuss how information can be transferred into knowledge to help agencies improve their operations.

6

KNOWLEDGE MANAGEMENT

INTRODUCTION

When the IFRC decided to include knowledge management as part of its preparedness strategy (see Chapter 3), it was because it understood that further competencies and value could be created from the lessons learned from previous disasters. The IFRC acknowledged that its supply chain would dramatically improve if it could capitalize on the knowledge possessed by the staff of the Red Cross Movement globally.

Every time a new team is deployed for an emergency, the IFRC, like any other global organization, learns something new about operating in a different part of the world. IFRC teams have to work with different partners and agencies, some of which may be in a country that is new to the team. They may have to abide by different religious rules or government procedures, and occasionally deal with different donors.

Knowledge is created not only within the organization, but also between organizations as they interact in the field. In fact, the maximum value of knowledge is produced only when it is captured and shared among the different stakeholders. Based on this, the UNJLC, like the

IFRC, has extended its information management function to capitalize on this shared knowledge.

The UNJLC's objective is to coordinate the efforts of humanitarian agencies, reduce duplication of efforts, and leverage resources (such as time, money, goods, transportation, human capital, etc.). Former Chief Information Officer Nigel Snoad comments on his experience dealing with disasters:

> *Basic information like fuel prices, road distances, flight schedules, or truck rates can easily be posted directly onto the website. It saves users time to have all that data centralized. However, the impact on the relief operation has been minimal when we have done this. Gathering and processing data to publish information is only half of our job, and the work would be incomplete if that is all we did ... The real goal is to disseminate knowledge that would drive the organizations to coordinate and become more efficient in light of limited resources and time pressures.*[1]

In this chapter, we explore how knowledge is created, at what levels it is needed, potential bottlenecks in collecting, processing, and disseminating it, and lastly the barriers to knowledge sharing.

HOW IS KNOWLEDGE CREATED?

Soon after the surrender of the Taliban forces in September 2002 a UNJLC team was deployed for the first time ever in Afghanistan.[2] They were to focus on the logistics and coordination issues for relief efforts. Upon arrival they quickly realized that most agencies were experiencing the same bottlenecks, yet there was little exchange of information and resources to overcome them. They encountered a typical scenario for emergencies where there was data overload, poor or unreliable information, little knowledge sharing, haphazard communication, and occasional, if any, interagency collaboration.

One of the initiatives of the UNJLC was to create a website through which field updates could be widely distributed. Snoad recalls,

> *In designing our information strategy, the goal was to support the UNJLC's coordination mandate. So our products had to be valuable and crucial in helping agencies to collaborate and coordinate their activities, reducing duplication of efforts, competition, cost of operation, and lead times. We needed to fill a gap in the humanitarian community by providing knowledge that would bridge their bottlenecks and improve efficiency.*

He goes on to say,

> *The task was not so simple. We were overloaded with data from many sources and a wish list of requests. We focused on logistics and began to process pieces of it to create information. The website and the bulletins had to be a one-stop point for information with clear and reliable recommendations for action that was quick to access.*

Through their trials and errors, the UNJLC team learned that good information did not necessarily translate into effective coordination. This would be achieved only if knowledge could facilitate collaboration and maximize the use of resources. With the goal of fostering collaboration, they agreed on a process that would collect data and turn

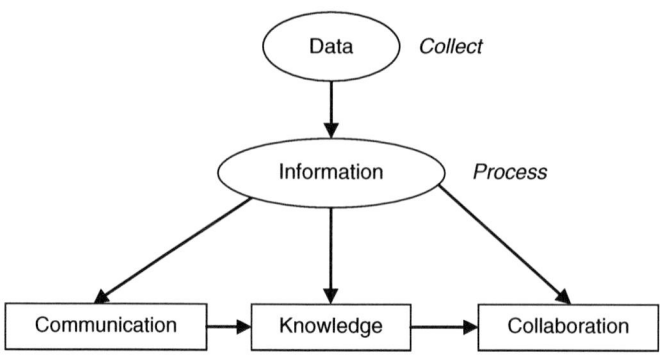

FIGURE 6.1 **Actionable Data Process**

it into information. Communication of this information would result in prompt action. It would also evolve into knowledge when interpreted based on previous experience. This shared knowledge would hopefully lead to better collaborative efforts (see Figure 6.1).

Data

Data is raw, unprocessed material such as facts and statistics that can be analyzed to produce information. The main problem with data collection is the potential for overload. Imagine driving down a transportation corridor in Afghanistan and trying to record every detail along the way, unaware of the purpose and usefulness of the data being collected. However, some data like the temperatures in the mountains during the winter can be very helpful.

Information

Information is data that has been given meaning, basically data processed in function of the context in which it is disseminated. It has a purpose and prompts action. It therefore needs to be timely, and in the format the recipient needs.

Information is crucial to maintaining and adapting competitive levels of resources (human and capital) and allowing officials to strategically plan their deployment.[3] This way donors and humanitarian agencies can, at different stages of the emergency, assess and deploy the right amount of funds, goods, and skills to the ground in a way that adds the most value without creating bottlenecks or inefficiencies.

Continuing with the Afghan winter example, the information created based on the raw temperature data dictates that access to the mountains will be blocked and additional resources will be needed to get people through the coldest months.

Communication

Exchange of information with a value statement equals communication. For instance, *"My stock of blankets has dropped to 10 units, I am going to be in trouble. There is a shooting in the main road corridor."* Much of this can be based on the interaction with locals, whose knowledge of the area and conditions can help to give a value statement to the information communicated. The value statement qualifies the implications of the information, often giving an indication of the actions required, as well as their urgency.

For example, in planning their winterization strategy for Afghanistan, humanitarians had to survey the locals to assess before the winter what the conditions would be like later on, and what factors should be considered for prepositioning goods.

Knowledge

Information becomes knowledge when know-how and staff expertise have been used to interpret it and make decisions. Much of this is based on the interpretation of experts or senior staff members.

For the Afghan winter example, this means that a food prepositioning strategy should be designed and executed before the winter to assist people in the high mountains.

Collaboration

Collaboration is when knowledge is equally shared and the parties are able to align their incentives to produce action. Following our example, the different agencies inter-act with suppliers and transport providers to implement the winterization strategy together in time.

KNOWLEDGE IS CREATED AND NEEDED AT DIFFERENT LEVELS

Indeed, knowledge is not exclusive to one layer of an organization, and should travel vertically and horizontally among the different components. In the case of a human-itarian supply chain, there are three main levels at which knowledge is created and needed: field, supply chain, and theater levels.

Field Operations Level: Knowledge Resides in the People

This level is the most people intensive, and in the case of humanitarian operations is often considered the main source of knowledge due to its proximity to the conditions and needs of the beneficiaries. Humanitarians in the field are in closest contact with needs, and thus are most informed and knowledgeable about priorities. However, it is one of the most challenging aspects to manage.

For example, in Afghanistan, the year one winterization strategy proved to be very successful. However, despite success the previous year, year two was a failure. How did that happen? It was very hard to implement a strategy in the second year because none of the staff from the previous year was still present in the country, and in most cases there had been no overlap and knowledge exchange between people coming in and those leaving. There was almost no transfer of experience at the organizational level and little knowledge was absorbed by the participating agencies to support the future operation. This is not a rare situation in a field with high staff turnover. People are oftentimes overworked, with limited resources and time, and are frequently pulled out of an operation abruptly, to be dragged cold into another emergency.

Supply Chain Level: Knowledge Resides in the Processes

At the supply chain level, knowledge transfer must be both vertical and horizontal; in other words, within the different levels of an organization as well as among the different organizations participating in the same supply chain. At this level, knowledge is extracted from the people to develop procedures, manuals, and standardized processes that can improve the performance of the supply chain.

The most popular and controversial example at this level is unsolicited donations. Following a disaster, the generosity of the international community is often manifested in many ways. Unfortunately, not all of the efforts are needed, and in fact, many of them create bottlenecks like the large number of planes with donations that arrived into Banda Aceh unsolicited following the Indian Ocean tsunami. For most of these planes, the humanitarian agencies were completely unaware of their content, and had to find a way to receive and offload them without forklifts or proper storage space. This strongly contributed to the creation of a huge bottleneck which significantly perturbed emergency relief operations.

Unsolicited donations can represent a major obstacle to the operation, taking up resources that could otherwise be used to provide better-quality assistance. Organizations have used their knowledge to develop lists of items needed per disaster type, and estimates for quantities, as well as specifications. They have also developed manuals and training modules to facilitate the processes and quality of delivery (norms for packaging, labeling, storage, loading, etc.).[4]

Knowledge can also be used to adapt product specifications to meet the needs more efficiently, for instance in defining survival kits. The content is not only a simplified and packaged solution, but kits take the responsibility away from the person who orders them on the minute details that should be included. For example, when someone orders an electricity kit, they will get a generator. The kit is packaged in such a way that a person who has never seen or used a generator before can easily figure out how to use it to meet his or her electricity needs. It will also include all the different fluids and accessories that could be needed, the type of things that a first timer ordering would most likely forget or not know about. Basically the kits are a way of packaging and passing on knowledge.

Theater Level: Knowledge Resides in the Context

This is the big picture level: for example, how do the physical, economic, or social conditions in the country or region affect operations? This could be knowledge about market conditions, regulatory measures, government dynamics, weather conditions, and so on. These are the factors of complexities discussed earlier in the book (see Chapter 2). Knowledge reduces complexity by helping to disentangle the issues affecting the supply chain.

The classic example is knowledge about the cultural context within the theater of operations. For example, while plastic blankets are considered to be warmer and longer lasting, there may be a cultural resistance by recipients who prefer natural fibers. Other examples are the segregation of the genders, awareness of the cast system, or dietary restrictions in communities practicing certain religions.

To highlight the interdependence of knowledge at different levels both within and among organizations, consider the fuel supplies situation in Iraq in 2003 (see Box 6.1[5]).

Box 6.1: UNJLC Fuel Forecasting in Iraq

John Levins, former Head of the Iraqi UNJLC Fuel Team explains,

In light of the potential for fuel disruptions to seriously affect transport and energy supply, our team had established a unique range of information resources from their own observations in the streets of Baghdad, Basra, and Erbil, to the Ministry of Oil itself, and daily situation Force reports from the US

Box 6.1: (Continued)

Army Corps of Engineers Task Force RIO (Restore Iraqi Oil). At the micro level, we spoke to Iraqi housewives waiting in line for liquid petroleum gas (LPG) for cooking and gauged how long people had to wait to refuel their cars. At the macro level, we tracked national production, imports, and tried to alert people that there was probably a lot more smuggling of oil products out of Iraq than was generally assumed.

Of course we could never repeat the Ministry or RIO sources verbatim, and we were always very careful not to publish information that could assist saboteurs, but we could summarize and analyze the information, link it with other things we knew, and make sense of it for our readership. For example, we were able to reinforce our conclusion that production of kerosene in the summer would be insufficient to build the necessary stockpiles and that imports would be necessary for the winter, and that LPG was a major issue, as was proved by the Basra riots months later. We tracked black market prices and our estimates of national demand were proved right when long queues of cars at Baghdad petrol stations disappeared once our estimates of overall supply matched our estimates of overall demand.

KNOWING AHEAD OF TIME

The whole idea behind developing and capturing knowledge focuses on value creation. In light of so much data, so many needs, and limited resources, the critical question for success is where to focus when developing knowledge. The decision takes into consideration the interaction between all three levels, and the mandates of the organizations concerned (which determines their priorities).

Former UNJLC Chief Operating Officer Adrian Van der Knaap comments on his organization's deployment process: *"At the beginning of an operation, our most important goal is to establish our credibility with our skills and expertise, and for that we need to convey good information and knowledge that is relevant to all."*

Knowledge takes time to develop and is a long-term investment that needs to be a part of organizational strategy. For example, the UNJLC is partially staffed by seconded individuals from other organizations. These include UN agencies, NGOs, military, donors, the private sector, and civil servants. This practice has enriched their pool of knowledge helping the UNJLC to understand the needs of the different stakeholders while absorbing the knowledge embodied in the persons themselves.

However, knowledge needs to produce immediate action. For that reason, on more critical issues UNJLC relies on experts to focus and process information that is crucial to the success of an operation ahead of time. This could be on a wide series of topics like the fuel case in Iraq discussed in Box 6.1, or regarding security, communications, customs, or air operations and logistics.

Expert knowledge can help identify bottlenecks and conflicts in advance with information already available, requiring minimal investment. Due to their specific knowledge, experts know what to look for, can help establish protocols ahead of time to collect information, analyze it, and communicate it to the community to take preventative actions. This mitigates and/or nullifies the impact of the bottlenecks and is proof of a positive and rising learning curve.

Another approach is to focus on modular or standardized processes and consult the specialist on their needs at each stage. A frequent example of these processes is air operations, for which there are widely accepted standardized procedures (e.g., size of the ramp, amount of fuel, operational security, air traffic control, loading and offloading, etc.). Having an air operations specialist available helps to identify ahead of time potential operational conflicts and requirements for optimization, and provides advice on how to manage the needs in light of the conditions on the ground.

THEY KNOW THAT YOU DON'T KNOW WHAT THEY KNOW... AND IT WILL COST YOU

In Afghanistan in 2002, as is often the case, agencies ended up competing at transportation hubs to hire trucks to take goods inland. There are not that many trucks, or truck drivers willing to make the trip due to security concerns. As a result there is intense competition among agencies.

Agencies without readily available cash (waiting for donors) are immediately out of the game since there are no credit terms in this transaction. As the competition intensifies, the cost per metric ton per kilometer increases. However, the worst element is that, in most cases, relief agencies have less than a full truck load to send – and they are not necessarily coordinating (sharing information) to consolidate their cargo. Thus they pay for empty space, hiking up the cost per ton shipped even more. Eventually, the truckers realize this lack of information sharing among the agencies and form a cartel which exponentially affects the transportation market in their favor.

Aware of their disadvantage, the humanitarian community agreed to collaborate by sharing information about prices, availability, and transportation needs to break the cartel. Formal meetings had to take place with the authorities to break it up, but in practice what needed to be done was to remedy the information asymmetry.

The UNJLC began to collect information and posted prices, helping to break the cartel. They then assisted agencies in centralizing information about their cargo transportation requirements and compared it with available truck capacity to help maximize the use of trucks (utilizing the excess capacity, sharing assets) at a reasonable rate.

BARRIERS TO KNOWLEDGE SHARING

Throughout this chapter we have highlighted the importance of sharing knowledge, but in practice this is rather difficult within and among organizations at the different levels. In this section we explore a few of the reasons why.

The challenge is to share knowledge so that it may become part of the organization (an asset/competency) and, most importantly, so that it be shared with the community (minimizing duplication of efforts). As with most relationships, parties are not willing or ready to share until they see a benefit from knowing what others know. Until then no one is willing to assume the cost/investment in sharing information.

Sharing is difficult for the following reasons:[6]

Knowledge is Power: So why share it? One of the spins is to make knowledge exchange a rewarding act by giving proper credit to the sources. Consider why a humanitarian organization would tell another that they have the cheapest rate to get aid into Afghanistan? The incentive may be to share space when they have less than a full truck load. An important point is to understand what power information provides, and when that power of information is useful to complete the necessary tasks.

Exchanging Knowledge Can Be Threatening: Organizations may be afraid of the negative repercussions of sharing knowledge about themselves. Revealing gaps or insufficiencies in the operations can reflect poorly on their performance. Rather than being penalized for their shortcomings, organizations need to be rewarded for revealing them and finding solutions in a collaborative way. For example, an organization may reveal gaps in their pipeline as an opportunity for others to share their stock and transportation.

Unknown Cost/Benefit Ratio: What is the value of knowledge and what is the effort needed to acquire it? How to know if the knowledge is a good deal if there is no way of knowing the value of what is circulated? There is a need to promote popular and relevant ideas. Eventually the usefulness and quality of the information will build a reputation that will attach a value to the source (as it is the case with most news agencies). This is how the UNJLC positions itself as a key player in knowledge management with the weekly bulletins posted on its website.

Knowledge is Contextual: The best knowledge resides where it was conceived, so how valuable would it be when transferred? There is a need to establish contact persons and promote dialogue and exchange. The key is to make that knowledge replicable and transferable to others. For this, the UNJLC had information managers that would be in frequent contact with people from different organizations in the field to understand the context.

Lack of Absorptive Capacity: How to avoid information overload? Focus on quality and relevance. Through constant validation of the priorities and regular feedback from the users one can focus on the most relevant aspects.

Knowledge Can Become Sacred: Knowledge becomes entrenched and hard to replace with new ideas and realities. Hence the need to stay on top of the latest developments and be ready to discard old ideas based on dated information. Keep in mind that crises and operations are dynamic with ever-changing needs and conditions.

CONCLUSION

High staff turnover and multiple crises happening simultaneously lead to an environment where there is little time to codify and transfer experiences. As a result many humanitarian organizations find themselves reinventing the wheel from one deployment to another, missing out on the valuable experiences of colleagues who perhaps lived through similar circumstances earlier.

As we discussed in Chapter 3, Knowledge Management is one of the key elements in making supply chain a core function of the organization. Increasingly we see organizations investing in this area as they become more aware of their shortcomings, redesign their processes, and prepare for the retirement of their most experienced and senior staff.

Though the knowledge produced within an organization is irreplaceable and extremely valuable, new sources of knowledge need to be considered to improve performance. In the next chapter we will be looking at private–humanitarian relations and the exchange of best practices.

7

BUILDING A SUCCESSFUL PARTNERSHIP

INTRODUCTION

In the previous chapters we have looked at different aspects of the humanitarian supply chain occasionally mentioning the role of the private sector and the potential for collaboration. This chapter specifically looks at how the two sectors can learn from each other through partnerships, and what are some of the challenges in setting them up. It also explains the process of transferring best practice, one of the main drivers for this type of cross-sector involvement.

PRIVATE–HUMANITARIAN PARTNERSHIPS

The reasons for the boom in cross-sector partnerships are simple: humanitarian organizations recognize that the private sector can help with resources and expertise, while the private sector is looking for opportunities to improve its impact on society through responsible actions. High-impact partnerships help to improve the competitive advantage of the parties involved. Such improvement comes as a result of the exchange of best practices and knowledge.

Companies have long supported humanitarian activities, either through commercial contracts or through philanthropic programs, but mostly in their home countries. However, in this era of rapid globalization of business, disasters like the Indian Ocean tsunami of 2004 have prompted companies to re-examine their roles and consider humanitarian activities in terms of their overall CSR strategy. By becoming better corporate citizens these companies believe they can benefit both their business and society, even though risks are involved.

Falling out of favor is the notion that just giving cash and in-kind donations to support humanitarian relief efforts is enough. Companies today are considering marrying short-term relief actions with longer-term disaster response partnerships with the humanitarian sector. When successful, these partnerships have the potential to exploit the core competencies of both business and humanitarian organizations, improve overall disaster preparedness, heighten corporate brand awareness, and, in some cases, contribute to disaster mitigation. They can also act as an effective forum for the exchange of information, ideas, and best practices that can improve efficiency and, in the case of the private sector, the bottom line. Partnerships also have the potential to deliver fast, effective support during a crisis, and can help build capacity between disasters.

Given the potential rewards of such cross-sector links, they are attracting increasing attention from both the corporate and the humanitarian sectors. Humanitarian organizations, which at one time regarded cash as the only useful form of corporate giving, are now recognizing that businesses have more to offer in terms of resources, expertise, and technology. As a result, they are becoming more open to discussions with the private sector and, in some instances, are identifying their ideal partners and making the first approach.

Similarly, companies are realizing that they may have something to learn from humanitarians, particularly about being agile and adaptable in difficult circumstances, one of the main strengths of humanitarian organizations. They too are manifesting an interest in initiating a cross-sector dialogue to examine what types of partnerships are feasible and most likely to deliver mutual benefits.

For an increasing number of companies these partnerships are also a visible means of demonstrating to their stakeholders, including employees, customers, vendors, and local communities that they actively subscribe to the concept of social responsibility. CSR has risen in importance over the years and is now an integral part of the business culture of a growing number of global companies. It is increasingly recognized as a key non-financial performance indicator that has the potential to affect a company's reputation as well as its share price.

For business to adopt an enhanced CSR strategy and expect to realize short-term business benefits in the face of long-term global needs may be unrealistic, but that does not lessen the importance of developing such a strategy for the long haul.

It was not until very recently that the private sector stepped in (cautiously and despite a lot of skepticism). Like every beginning, the road has not been easy. While the private sector may be relatively independent of politics, it functions with incentives different from those of the humanitarian sector, like making profit rather than saving lives.

BUILDING LEARNING LABS

The emergence of CSR has made corporations more aware of the potential gains in areas rarely considered before. Michael Porter[1] argues that corporations can enhance their competitiveness by engaging in partnerships where social and economic values overlap. In an attempt to do just that, many private sector logistics companies – including TNT, DHL, UPS, FedEx, and Agility – have identified a match between their competencies and activities and those of humanitarian aid agencies that specialize in emergency relief.

The aftermath of the 2004 Indian Ocean tsunami amply demonstrated that logistics plays a substantial role in delivering aid in emergencies. The circumstances and settings are very different from private sector logistics, yet they present attractive learning opportunities for private sector partners. For example, companies increasingly need the same sort of skills as relief organizations, given the dynamic demands and disruption risks of operating global supply chains and the central role of logistics in increasing profits when it comes to short-term changes in demand or supply (agility), or in adjusting their design to market changes in the medium term (adaptability). As a result, corporations have realized that while high speed and low cost may be necessary for a successful supply chain, they are not sufficient to ensure a competitive and sustainable advantage over rivals. Such advantage comes only when the supply chain is also agile, adaptable, and aligned.[2]

Unlike the private sector, humanitarian organizations are specialists in being agile and adaptable, implementing complex supply chains under high levels of uncertainty, with limited resources and infrastructure, and often overnight.

Private logistics companies increasingly participate in partnerships with humanitarian organizations, approaching the latter not only with a charitable intent but also as an opportunity for learning and business development. In a partnership every joint project either between or during a disaster is an opportunity to learn. Done well, these partnerships can become learning labs for both parties. Humanitarian agencies invest equal resources, hoping to enhance their performance and core competencies through interaction with their private sector partners. In operational terms, the humanitarians can mainly benefit from their partners in two particular areas: back-office support for better disaster preparedness, and the movement of key assets during a crisis (food donations, medicines, shelters, or telecommunications equipment).

Back-Office Support

Pedro Figueredo, WFP Regional Logistics Coordinator, emphasizes that in emergency operations *"The concern among logistics firms and relief agencies is that we can't feed the beneficiaries or transport the food to them. It's a race against time in the sense that the ports, railways, roads, warehouses and silos all need to be coordinated."* This type of complex and large-scale coordination is neither improvised nor coincidental. In fact, Bernard Chomilier, former Head of Logistics at the IFRC, explains that *"To be prepared, humanitarians need to work not only during disasters but, more importantly, between disasters, developing agreements and establishing policies and processes to operate swiftly during disasters with existing as well as new supply chain partners."*

Between disasters, alignment, as an aspect of preparedness, is one area in which the private sector is able to transfer its knowledge and expertise to the humanitarian sector. Indeed, it has long focused on strengthening relationships with its partners and establishing incentives to improve the performance of the whole supply chain. This includes negotiating agreements with suppliers and service providers, and implementing tools that can provide greater visibility, facilitate communications and reporting, and enable better planning and forecasting.

Humanitarians in the Forefront

The front-office activities of the actual relief operation in a crisis remain in the hands of the humanitarian agencies, as that is their core competency and primary role. Humanitarian organizations are licensed to operate in conflict zones and disaster areas thanks to their guiding principles of humanity, impartiality, and neutrality, which aim to create a space in which they can operate free of political and economic agendas. But in light of their other stakeholders (donors, the military, governments, suppliers, carriers, implementing partners, and beneficiaries), such a task can be a real challenge. It is important to have systems and processes in place that can facilitate collaboration among stakeholders to keep efficiency at high levels. Help from the private sector can be invaluable here. However, it is also crucial to minimize undesirable outcomes that could contradict humanitarian principles. Therefore, it is better if the military and the private sector do not get actively involved in running relief operations at the scene of the disaster.

Emergencies test the reactivity and capacity of the relief agencies, and often overwhelm them in the first few days.

During an emergency relief operation private sector partners can assist the humanitarian agencies with readily accessible assets (e.g., airplanes, forklifts, office and warehouse space, call centers, telecommunications equipment) and skills (e.g., programmers, communication specialists, pilots) to meet demand in the field. This may be pro bono or at cost, helping to keep the overall expense of the operation down and enhancing speed in the first few days of a response.

FORMS OF CORPORATE SUPPORT FOR HUMANITARIAN ACTIVITIES

Being a good corporate citizen is at the heart of most companies' humanitarian activities, whether this revolves around providing cash, goods, human resources, knowledge and expertise, or a combination of these, each with its pros and cons (as indicated below). Typically, support is provided immediately after a disaster, although there may be a significant disaster preparedness component in some corporate initiatives.

Cash

Cash is still the most important, and often the most appropriate, donation for humanitarian relief and recovery efforts, enabling humanitarian agencies to purchase essential goods and services upfront, mainly relief supplies and transportation. From the corporate point of view the advantage of cash is that the expense is defined, but it also has other less-tangible benefits in terms of return-on-investment. For example, fund-raising activities organized by employees (and inspired by a corporate promise to match the amount raised) can be more effective than other more conventional team-building events. The downside of donating cash is that it requires a certain amount of due diligence on the company's part to determine that the humanitarian agency chosen to receive the cash has a track record in the disaster area (capability), and can provide reliable data about how it manages its funds (accountability).

Goods

When appropriate, in-kind donations may be a useful alternative to cash in the aftermath of a disaster. For example, Ericsson, the international communications company, provided mobile phones to humanitarian workers following the Indian Ocean tsunami, while Danone, the French-based food company, donated bottled mineral water. However, companies often fail to realize that in-kind donations should be based on demand, as specified either by the government of the affected country or by a recognized humanitarian agency with existing operations in the disaster area, rather than on what they can supply.

Unsolicited donations cause bottlenecks and needless expenditure. For example, it took six months to burn the unwanted donations received during Eritrea's 1989 war, including seven truckloads of expired aspirin. The key is for companies to work closely with aid agencies, local embassies, or possibly a supply chain partner in the region, rather than launching their own mini-NGO.

Volunteers

Volunteers from the corporate sector, like in-kind donations, may also hinder rather than help relief efforts if the people volunteering are not equipped with the relevant skills, expertise, or knowledge. Technical competence and noble intentions alone are not enough. Volunteers also need to be familiar with the local context, have experience with emergency situations, and preferably fluency in the language of the country in order to be effective from the outset.

Partnerships

Corporate–humanitarian partnerships that share knowledge, expertise, and best practices can result in more efficient ways of dealing with disaster responses, aid distribution, and, especially, disaster preparedness and disaster mitigation. They have significant potential to deliver benefits across the board to the partners and to the people and communities affected by a disaster. But setting up these partnerships and making them work effectively raises many issues and challenges.

CSR PARTNERSHIP CHALLENGES

Most of the obstacles to successful cross-sector partnerships result from the cultural differences between sectors. In a 2005 study of 25 humanitarian organizations carried out by INSEAD,[3] five main concerns surfaced:

- *Lack of mutual understanding*
- *Lack of transparency and accountability*
- *Level of commitment*
- *Roles and responsibilities*
- *Relationship management*

Lack of Mutual Understanding

Given their different working environments and objectives, each sector has its own context. Take, for example, the partnership between TNT, the global transportation and logistics company based in The Netherlands, and the WFP. While TNT and WFP may have logistics in common, they each have their own ways of going about it, with different goals and objectives (speed, cost, lives saved, beneficiaries, etc.) and decision-making processes (more or less bureaucracy or political sensitivity). These diverging notions of logistics can create undesirable bottlenecks in the system when they work together.

Solution: Specify requests and needs so that contribution channels are predefined and expectations are met when and where needed, according to the most pressing needs. The best time to do this is during non-emergency periods as a means to enhance preparedness and as the potential partner is more free to explain their needs and concerns. During emergencies it may be too late, too improvised.

Lack of Transparency and Accountability

Motivation for engagement is a gray area of CSR where commercial and philanthropic intentions can easily overlap. The line between the two is fuzzy and can create a conflict of interest between organizations that have not fully agreed on their position in the engagement spectrum (see Figure 7.1). The resulting confusion can lead to understatement, but more often overstatement, of the contribution. If the private sector and humanitarian organizations find themselves in a position where they have to

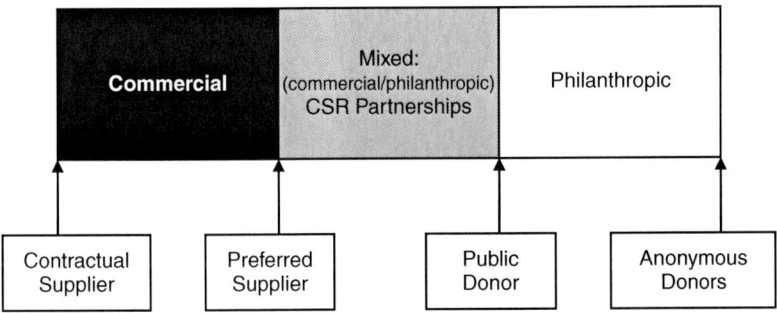

FIGURE 7.1 **The Engagement Spectrum**

compete for airtime and media exposure, collaboration will simply not work.

Each sector has different values, responds to different stakeholders, and protects its image and reputation in different ways to maintain its license to operate. Humanitarian organizations generally want to remain as neutral and impartial as possible from political and economic agendas, while business wants to be seen creating the highest impact through their involvement.

Solution: Agree on responsible public relations and communication strategies to avoid conflicting messages that could compromise the validity of either party. Different strategies can be defined for different levels of engagement in the spectrum (see Box 7.1).

Box 7.1: Engagement Spectrum (see Figure 7.1)

Companies have different motivations for engaging with humanitarian agencies. At different points the motivation will define how parties approach the engagement. Following are a few examples:

Box 7.1: (Continued)

Purely commercial relations (at the far left of the spectrum) will be managed by both parties through the traditional processes for procurement (e.g., request for quotation) and are regulated by contractual agreements. This relationship is subject to market conditions and is based on the expressed needs of the humanitarian organization soliciting the goods or services. Some parties in the commercial sector may want to become a preferred supplier and thus compromise on some terms to build longer relations (e.g., invest more in getting to know their clients' business and/or provide better terms, to engage in longer contracts).

Purely philanthropic relations (at the far right of the spectrum) such as anonymous donors will be handled by the communications and PR departments and eventually incorporated into the organization as they see fit (e.g., money raised through an event can be put into a fund and then distributed). Some donors may be seeking a greater value from their contribution and thus see an interest in going public with their actions. Publicity enhances their brand and reputation as well as employee motivation, while positioning the company as a good corporate citizen with minimum involvement (e.g., companies sponsoring school programs or donating resources, while publicizing the fact by using their logo and following up with their PR department).

The gray area (in the middle of the spectrum) is where the commercial and philanthropic motives mix and where the rules of engagement still have to be determined. The combination of motives raises concerns such as commitment, transparency and accountability, lack of mutual understanding, need for relationship management, and a better definition of roles and responsibilities.

Keep in mind that this spectrum represents interaction points for both sectors. Companies may choose to have multiple interaction points. For example, they may establish a CSR partnership that is public but also have programs that are purely commercial (e.g., supplying services on a commercial basis) and solicit anonymous contributions from employees. The only problem with this mixture is that it may involve a conflict of interest. For example, by engaging in pro bono work with a humanitarian organization the company may gain substantial knowledge and thus be in a better position to bid for tender on the commercial side. To avoid potential scandals, companies must be aware of their various interaction points and raise "Chinese walls" (protective barriers) around the pools of shared knowledge.

Commitment at All Levels

Humanitarian organizations often see their partner fully motivated and engaged at the C-suite level but experience little buy-in from the rest of the organization. This poses a major problem given that partnerships often start from the top down but grow from the bottom up when the operational levels work out ways to collaborate and transcend their differences. Contact at the operational level provides an excellent opportunity to validate the needs and solutions upon which interaction channels will be built.

Jean-Jacques Graisse, a senior official with the WFP, claims that *"There are no forgotten emergencies, just emergencies that donors choose not to fund."* The same holds true for private sector involvement. Officials working for humanitarian organizations often comment that some of the world's greatest humanitarian needs are found in areas where neither the media nor the private sector have dared to venture. For the most part, assistance follows the CNN or BBC trail. This can be frustrating for agencies that want to prioritize their actions based on needs rather than return-on-investment. In practice, it means that if a company pledges resources, the humanitarian managers should be sure that they can be deployed regardless of media presence, location, or local conditions. Unfortunately, the greatest needs today are found in neglected areas of the world where access, poverty, and security can be an issue.

Solution: Develop engagement rules that define the needs in advance and can be fulfilled by the partnership, along with protocols and guidelines to agree on service levels, and clarify expectations at the different levels and stages.

Roles and Responsibilities

Agencies may be reluctant to let private partners take on responsibilities that are critical for their operation or in areas where they feel they can do it best themselves (e.g., deploying the first post-disaster team and flying in the first round of goods in the midst of chaos). Likewise, companies want to get involved in areas that are relatively low

cost and easy for them to do with relatively high visibility
(e.g., sending their excess inventory into a disaster area
as quickly as possible while the cameras are still rolling,
regardless of how it may fit the needs on the ground). As
a result, many opportunities to work together fail, duplication of effort occurs, and each contribution carries a high
transaction cost to both parties.

Solution: Determine areas to leverage respective competencies and allow each party to focus on where they make
the highest impact from their contribution, rather than
each one trying to do the most (or the most visible) at every
point.

Relationship Management

Lack of an interface to enforce protocols and regulations
creates further confusion about when and how to engage
with each other. The interface needs to be designed to
build trust, foster mutual respect, and develop a common
language and goals.

For example, vehicle fleet management is the second largest cost in the humanitarian sector after human
resources. While transport companies have a lot of knowledge and experience in this area that they could transfer
to humanitarians, doing so requires an interface that can
bridge the cultural differences between the two. Initiatives
like the Fleet Forum[4] allow humanitarian organizations and
the private sector to interact via a broker for best results.
Rob McConnell, former Fleet Forum Coordinator, recalls
an experience where a well-known vehicle manufacturer
offered to conduct an analysis on road safety for some
humanitarian agencies. As the broker, McConnell had to
ensure that the company would not interpret the lack of

data as a lack of interest on behalf of the humanitarian agencies. On the contrary, it was a sign that this was an area in need of support.

Solution: Develop partnerships in non-emergency periods rather than during emergencies (when it may be too late). Building the relationship and getting to know each other requires significant investment on both sides. Pre-negotiated collaboration minimizes the risk of mistakes, false assumptions, and potential confusion, and provides an opportunity for the partners to establish clearer expectations.

INVESTING IN PARTNERSHIPS: THE TNT–WFP CASE[5]

Despite the fundamental differences between the two sectors, partnerships through CSR can and do work out in ways beneficial for both parties. One example is TNT and the WFP on their joint venture Moving the World.

Since 2002, TNT – a global provider of mail, express, and logistics services that serves more than 200 countries – has been an active partner of the WFP, the world's largest humanitarian aid agency. Each year WFP provides food aid to an average of 90 million people, including 56 million hungry children, in more than 80 countries.

TNT has committed its knowledge, skills, and resources to helping WFP for a minimum of five years. In 2004 alone, TNT invested a total of €8.5 million in the partnership, of which €7 million came in the form of in-kind services and knowledge transfer projects, and €1.5 million as cash donations. For 2005, TNT had upped its commitment to €10 million in knowledge transfer, hands-on support, and funding and awareness initiatives.

How It Began

In November 2001, during a flight to Singapore, TNT's CEO Peter Bakker read an article on the increasing gap between the rich and the poor. Even though there is enough food in the world to feed everyone, every five seconds a child dies from hunger. He could not help feeling that in emergency situations, hunger was, to a large extent, a logistics problem.

Bakker realized that TNT, with over 160,000 employees in 63 countries, was in a unique position to make a contribution to solving this problem. He immediately emailed his idea to a small group of senior TNT managers from Strategy, Development, Corporate Communications, and HR divisions. Within a few hours all the recipients had replied positively, and with conviction they began to brainstorm the notion of developing a CSR program on a global scale.

TNT had already sponsored numerous local, relatively small-scale initiatives and community programs around the world, as well as a high-profile annual golf tournament in The Netherlands. *"These initiatives had met their objectives, and in 2001 it was time to initiate programs in line with TNT's global presence,"* noted Ludo Oelrich, Program Director for Moving the World.

The Four Steps in Partner Selection

Step One: Finding a Focus
For Bakker and his management team it was a question of whether to focus internally or externally on the topic of environment or people. Bakker believed that *"It's not enough to be socially responsible within our company. We should*

strive for social leadership outside our business. If through our business we can help improve people's living conditions, it is our responsibility to do so."

Focusing externally would give TNT's employees a stronger sense of belonging and pride in doing something valuable while doing their work. For the management team, focusing on people outside the company translated into humanitarian work. Establishing a presence in the humanitarian landscape would position TNT as a people-focused company that could make a difference in society. It was also a way of broadening its relations with the different stakeholders that could affect its business, including non-private–sector players like NGOs, advocacy groups, government, civil society, and the press.

Step Two: Filtering Candidates

In the non-profit sector, each organization has a different structure, funding mechanism, mandate, ideology, and modus operandus. TNT realized that it was not possible to compare humanitarian organizations in a fair and objective manner using standard business indicators. This made it difficult to rank the candidates and determine the best fit for TNT.

To filter suitable candidates, TNT focused on reputation and neutrality. A potential partner's reputation had to be commensurate with TNT's global scale and have a similar tone and message. It was important that the partner reflect TNT's international presence without inhibiting its ability to do business globally. While many humanitarian organizations had compatible global presence and recognition, their ideological stand on controversial issues could compromise the company's image. TNT took the position that it was more neutral to focus on food and education for children, which is to a large extent a logistics issue, rather than engage in a political debate about issues like child labor and exploitation, prostitution, or human trafficking. For example, TNT was trying to bolster its presence in China. Partnering with an organization deeply rooted in human rights could have had an unintended negative impact on TNT's business license there. The same rationale would hold true for faith-based organizations, despite their goodwill and positive reputation. Only a combination of good reputation and neutrality could ensure the program would be well received and adopted in every country where TNT was known.

Step Three: Candidate Selection

Having developed a list of compatible humanitarian organizations, the management team began to look at "organizational fit" between TNT and the candidates; that is, how their core competencies matched and how compatible their strategies would be for the future. Through a detailed review of TNT's strategy and attributes, the management team came up with four weighted criteria: matching competencies (40%), PR value/interest and attitude (30%), effectiveness/overhead cost (20%), and geographic scope (10%).

- *Matching Competencies*: TNT intended to share its logistics knowledge and capabilities, rather than just donate cash. Logistics had to be of great value to the candidates so that TNT's contribution would be welcomed and appreciated.
- *Public Relations Value*: The partner organization needed to share TNT's vision and have similar global brand exposure. Basically, the two brands needed to be compatible and add value to each other.

- *Effectiveness and Overhead Cost*: It was important that any partner mirror TNT's culture for successful action-driven operations. *"The last thing we wanted to do was to get involved with an organization consumed by bureaucracy,"* explained TNT's Ludo Oelrich.
- *Geographic Scope*: This was factored in to determine the outreach potential of the efforts.

These selection criteria narrowed the search to five strong candidates. Each was approached by TNT to participate in a second round of enquiries.

Step Four: Comparing Candidates
TNT believed that it was important to give the candidates an opportunity to voice their needs and check how they matched TNT's capabilities, rather than just selling how TNT could help them. During this process TNT realized not only how little it knew about the humanitarian sector, but also how little the humanitarian sector knew about the company. To overcome this information shortfall, TNT opened the meetings by briefly presenting a company overview focusing on its capabilities. To objectively compare the five agencies, TNT developed a template detailing five main criteria: organizational fit, image/interest and attitude, marketing and communications, logistics, and opportunities.

- *Organizational Fit*: This covered an overview of the candidate's structure, size, areas of operations, services provided, costs, income sources, and growth rate and potential.

- *Image/Interest and Attitude*: This looked at detailed descriptions of potential partners' image and political engagement.
- *Marketing and Communications*: This included a list of VIPs associated with the marketing efforts of possible partners. TNT also evaluated the value and possibilities of shared marketing and communications in a partnership.
- *Logistics*: Candidates were asked to describe their current practices, skills and knowledge, types of goods distributed, sources used, destinations, types of transport, timelines involved, and overall logistics flow.
- *Opportunities*: Candidates had a chance to express what they envisioned as opportunities for the future, having been asked to outline their outstanding logistical and advisory needs.

After approximately four months of searching, TNT was able to rank the finalists and confirm an organizational fit with a small group of agencies. Before they would commit to one, they invested even more time in confirming the emotional fit (commitment, shared vision, enthusiasm), and organizational readiness of the candidates to engage in such a large project. Two months later they partnered with the UN WFP.

Making it Work in the Long Term

While finding the right organizational fit is critical, equally important in the long-range sustainability of any partnership is the emotional fit between the two organizations.

At their first meeting with former WFP Executive Director Jim Morris, TNT's Bakker and Oelrich confirmed there was indeed an emotional fit. Bakker recalled, "*Morris showed strong signs of commitment and motivation, pointing out the many areas in which WFP could benefit from TNT's expertise. Most important, we recognized in him the same driving values and vision that guided us in our partner search process.*" Morris had joined the agency after many years in the private sector and understood the benefits and opportunities for WFP in its partnership with TNT. He voiced this with enthusiasm and seemed to share TNT's level of conviction and commitment.

Bakker and Morris understood that such a partnership would require significant investment and that it would potentially change the way they each did business. It was important for both to know how ready each organization was to change and grow through the partnership. During their first meeting, Morris explained WFP's logistics agenda, revealing areas in which the UN agency could benefit from TNT's help. This validated the fact that WFP was ready to assume change and cooperate on an equal basis with a partner. It made it easier for both to envision the future.

Establishing Interaction Channels

Once the organizational and emotional fits are confirmed, the next step is to establish interaction channels to enable both partners to define tangible, realistic projects with clear goals. During this step, both management teams should develop a sense of identity with the program to help the partnership grow beyond the minds of the initial leaders.

TNT and WFP decided to carry out this step during a retreat in Tanzania with members of the senior management team from different business units. They visited refugee camps, school feeding programs, and regional emergency relief projects. They interacted with victims of political unrest, people with HIV/AIDS, and a large number of orphans, witnessing extreme poverty in areas that had limited access to vital resources, care, and education.

The TNT team began to understand that the main elements of emergency logistics were high uncertainty, limited resources (both human and capital), and an extreme sense of urgency. This was the chance for TNT to explain how its core competencies could add value. TNT summarized its ideas at the end of the retreat and both organizations agreed on five interaction channels. It was now up to TNT's management to build the business case for the partnership and get the support of the board.

Building the Business Case

Following the retreat, Oelrich made a presentation to the TNT board explaining the need for the partnership, the candidate search process, and the potential benefits of choosing WFP. He made the point that the partnership would not involve cash donations but rather an exchange of capabilities and expertise that would improve TNT's own long-term competitiveness in the industry.

While it was difficult to show a formula (or even an estimate), or to calculate the return-on-investment, the presentation assured the board of the potential gains from the program. The response was positive enough to move forward with rational skepticism. To guarantee a fair shot, Oelrich engaged the board even more by asking the members to personally adopt an initiative and to devote time into its development. They all agreed.

Keeping the Momentum

Once a partnership is up and running, keeping and growing the partnership and its momentum becomes critical to success. Expect hurdles.

Be Open and Honest on Both Sides

Openness should be practiced from the beginning of the selection process, and especially when validating the different fits. Once the partnership is signed and the whole organization gets involved, one should expect unforeseen challenges through the interaction. Two partners need to dance at the same pace, to the same tune, without stepping on each other's toes; above all to be able to enjoy it while the crowd is watching.

As TNT and WFP learned to dance, they realized that inherently they had two different speeds: an efficiency-driven logistics company with long-term plans versus a large bureaucratic organization with a short-term planning horizon. Moreover, they spoke two different organizational languages: one emphasizing directness and action, the other diplomacy. As the partnership was unprecedented for both sectors, Moving the World was closely watched (by cynics inside and outside both organizations), adding to the pressure to succeed. Today, TNT and WFP acknowledge that they are two different organizations who over time have learned to dance together without losing their respective identities. They also acknowledge they have a long way to go before they can win a professional dance competition.

Learn the Dynamics: Measure, Evaluate Critically, Adapt/Adjust

As the challenges emerge, the important thing is to remain focused and flexible. Therefore projects should not only have a natural fit in the interaction channels, but both parties should also agree on the benefits expected. This way projects can be measured with indicators that are relevant to both partners and maintain mutual interest. The ultimate goal through this process is to have the initiatives become a part of daily business.

Instead of competing with a company's daily business activities, CSR projects should become a part of the way a company conducts business. After all, when managers allocate portions of their budget to different projects, they evaluate the opportunity cost. Without a clear value proposition and measurement system CSR projects will be viewed as incidental and fall out of the priority list. A manager who is not sure about letting his best people go to a rotational assignment on a CSR project could argue, *"Why spend money outside the company when you would rather increase your assets or staff with a similar amount of money or less... what is in it for me?"* For this reason, CSR projects should have a "strategy map" and a "scorecard" that reflect and measure the actions vis-à-vis the company's overall business strategy.

Spread Ownership Internally and Communicate Successes
The program needs to be anchored solidly in lower management ranks, not just at the C-suite level. The scorecard approach enables different business units to have greater ownership and accountability of the initiatives. As a tool, it will help them identify their contribution to the overall strategy of the company through their participation in the program.

The glow of media attention and increased brand awareness are not enough to sustain a partnership on this scale. Eventually, media and other stakeholders, especially those for whom social value is not the primary purpose of investing in a company, will demand results beyond the public relations value. If these results are not forthcoming, things can quickly backfire.

Internally and externally it is important to communicate the achievements of the program to overcome skepticism among those seeking immediate results. CSR is a long-term investment that requires perseverance. In the meantime, one needs to nurture the expectations and goodwill of all those involved to sustain the momentum.

VALUE THROUGH LEARNING

Many humanitarian–private collaborations have been designed under the CSR umbrella to exchange best practices as a means to enhance the partners' performance. Through the exchange process each partner builds new knowledge from the learning steps, ultimately creating social and economic value for their sector.

However, creating value through the exchange of best practices demands attention and resources. Successful partnerships have taken this investment seriously with special attention to overcoming the barriers to exchange best practices. When properly done, these exchanges can develop new knowledge in the organizations through the learning process they initiate.

LEARNING: A DIFFICULT PROCESS THAT NEEDS TO BE MANAGED PROACTIVELY

In a field driven by goodwill (humanitarianism), is "willingness" enough to learn from one another? Unfortunately, the answer is "no." Learning needs to be managed proactively, with the right mixture of resources, motivation, and incentives for it to create sustainable value. Informal and casual exchanges will not suffice to replicate knowledge in different settings.

For example, transport providers travel the same routes, trying to reach areas in need. They face similar bottlenecks including difficult weather, challenging road conditions, security concerns, questions of fuel availability, and maintenance needs. While in transit, drivers share the same guesthouses and restaurants. Inevitably, informal networks develop through which information and advice are exchanged (e.g., the road is too muddy you may get stuck, security is weak in that corridor). But these informal networks lack an organized system that proactively captures and transfers best practices. Therefore, learning is haphazard at best.

The example above addresses learning at the personal level through the exchange of best practices. Yet, learning can happen at many different levels within an organization, between organizations, or between sectors. Here, we focus on the interaction between sectors (humanitarian and private).

Learning Proposition

The business case for learning is well received today as one of the drivers of CSR. Leading companies are applying their resources to solve chronic social problems as a means to stimulate their own business development.[6] This type of investment is often done through partnerships that leverage core competencies and exchange best practices through pre-established channels.

For example, humanitarian organizations have begun to welcome additional expertise and capacity from the private sector to reduce their costs and increase their speed of response. Similarly, private companies are eager to learn from the agility and adaptability shown by humanitarians responding to unpredictable, large-scale disasters like a tsunami or an earthquake.

The humanitarian sector is driven by unpredictable needs, thus continuity is a big issue. When the majority of organizational resources, human and capital, are devoted to disaster response (or "front office"), little is left to invest in knowledge exchange. The private sector, therefore, has an opportunity to help humanitarians work more efficiently between disasters, with back-office support to improve their response capacity.

Challenging Humanitarian Learning

To create value in a partnership, both parties need to focus on intense interaction channels. To increase the potential success of these channels, it is essential to ensure that both partners are able to

1. Identify and codify each other's best practices relevant to the needs of the partnership.
2. Recognize and prioritize best practices (solutions) that are generic enough to be transferred.
3. Allocate resources and set incentives for the exchange of best practices.
4. Invest in developing routines for the transfer.

In establishing these channels, consider the following:

Do I know what I know?

The fast-pace environment of humanitarian operations and its high staff turnover have led to a situation in which many humanitarian organizations are only vaguely aware of "what" they are best at, and "why." Before they can consider transferring or acquiring knowledge, it is essential that both parties understand their own best practices.

Would that work?

The lack of standardization in the humanitarian sector, coupled with the diversity of organizational structures (e.g., UN fund or program, federations, committees, consortia), makes it difficult to identify best practices that can be easily transferred. Even then, few practices would be considered generic enough to be adopted system-wide. For example, attempts are being made to incorporate "category management" into the humanitarian supply chain. This practice, with a long track record in the private sector, groups items based on demand in the same category (e.g., toothpaste, toothbrush, mouthwash). Agencies are currently seeking to define these categories and could benefit from the private sector's experience with this exercise.

Can we transfer that?

Even when the practice can be deemed generic enough, a key success factor is making sure the practice is well transferred. This means setting up interaction channels between the two partners, with resources and incentives to drive the exchange. Both parties need to understand why the practice works and its value to each one of them. They also need to develop a plan to implement the practice in the new setting, and monitor its performance until it is fully integrated.

All or nothing!?
Unfortunately, there is no gradual transfer of best practice. The practice is either fully replicated or it is not. Unless the parties exchanging practices are fully engaged until the end, the benefit will not be obtained.

BARRIERS TO EXCHANGE BEST PRACTICE

Success depends on how well both parties learn from each other. In these cases, learning is the process of developing knowledge that is embedded in the best practices transferred. The challenge is how to reduce the barriers between two different sectors and create a system to effectively exchange best practices.

The difference between the two sectors should not be a deterrent for learning or best practice transfer. Research[7] shows that the "not-invented-here" syndrome is not the biggest barrier to learning. In fact, statistics reveal that arduous relations, causal ambiguity, and absorptive capacity are far greater barriers. Consider the following statement as we review the barriers in the following sections:

> *I may be very motivated and willing to learn but we are 5,000km apart and do not meet regularly (arduous relationship). I don't really understand what these other guys are doing and why it works for them (causal ambiguity). I am constantly over-stressed (limited absorptive capacity) so transferring a best practice from them to me is not going to work.*

1. *Arduous Relations*: Ease of communications and intimacy of the overall relationship.

Cultural gaps have been shaped by stereotypes that inhibit the trust between parties. For example, humanitarians exist to save lives, while the private sector is focused on making money. To save lives, humanitarians are willing to go into dangerous areas at any time and for any length of time, while the private sector may not go the same distance (or will simply go as far as the cameras will follow).

When TNT's CEO Peter Bakker was asked what he had learned two years into the partnership with the WFP, he replied, *"Businesses are not humanitarian agencies."* His statement reinforces the idea that saving lives is a humanitarian job, and the role of business is to provide a support function to humanitarian operations.

Clearly defined roles and expectations help to break the barriers of stereotypes, but nothing surpasses the benefits of networking and personal relationships. Not surprisingly, several humanitarians expressed that, under pressure, they are more likely to call upon people they know well or at least have met personally.
Solutions:

- Establish an interface to share experiences with other organizations and understand each other's culture, incentives, and priorities.
- Develop ambassadors, at different levels, to help bridge the communication gaps and demystify the differences between the two organizations.

2. *Causal Ambiguity*: When the reasons for success or failure in replicating a best practice in a new setting cannot be determined.
   Transferring best practices is not about acquiring new knowledge but about taking advantage of existing

knowledge. As such, it is important to separate the key elements that make a practice successful from the context in which it occurs. For example, the similarities between warehousing in a disaster area and a European distribution center are not always immediately obvious. Such was the case with TNT, when they were asked to help redesign humanitarian warehousing in Brindisi. TNT transferred their vast knowledge of commercial warehousing, while at the same time gained knowledge of the complexity of humanitarian operations.

Later on, TNT was also requested to examine the distribution network in war-torn South Sudan. The transfer of best practices was less obvious due to the complexity of the situation. After 20 years of fighting, primary access to the area was by air, and new roads had to be built to bring in aid by land at a more sustainable cost. The TNT team required more in-depth analysis before they were able to deliver a reasonable contribution to the UN. The challenge to transfer the knowledge was an opportunity for TNT to refine their knowledge in a new setting with new conditions.

Solutions:

- Encourage the exchange and secondment of staff to execute tasks where responsibility and risk are shared.
- Build a common language and use it to reframe one another's needs. This will allow partners to embrace commonalities while becoming more aware and respectful of differences.
- Communicate and evaluate with your partner the internal applications of the lessons learned from the experiences.

3. *Absorptive Capacity*: Inability to exploit outside sources of knowledge.

Humanitarians invest the majority of their capacity in attending to disasters with limited human and capital resources, numerous uncertainties, and scarce information. Partnerships can be created to alleviate constraints and improve performance with additional resources and expertise. However, partnerships have a high absorption cost too, which may be counterproductive during disasters. Based on their limited resources, many NGOs have decided not to divert their attention to partnering with the private sector, or to do so through a third party who will manage their private sector relations.

Solutions:

- Discuss priorities and the allocation of resources to interaction channels with your partners ahead of time and assess the resources that will be needed from both to work together.
- Develop indicators, with reasonable expectations, to measure the progress of the transfer. Use this to assess continuous improvement throughout the transfer process.
- Recognize that there can be multiple benefits during the learning process, so be open to embracing unexpected positive outcomes. Keep in mind that there is no single method of learning.

CONCLUSION

Throughout this book we have been mentioning the learning opportunities that private–humanitarian partnerships offer. In this chapter we have discussed the process of establishing them, the need to identify roles and responsibilities, and ways of making them sustainable. More importantly, we have discussed the need to focus on learning as a central element of partnerships.

Much like establishing partnerships, learning is a difficult process that needs to be managed proactively with the right resources and motivation. Neither partnership nor learning can succeed without well thought-out, mutually agreed interaction channels.

For interaction to be productive and result in learning for both parties, managers must determine which needs the interaction channels will address. They must also consider why and how suitable their best practices are to addressing those needs. Partners must then work together to build an effective relationship, while keeping in mind that there are many ways of learning, and that during the learning process unexpected benefits are likely to emerge that will help the partnership grow.

Partnerships, however, are not for everyone. They require a substantial investment and encompass a broad set of risks which have not been addressed here. For some companies, and in some circumstances, less engagement is, in fact, more, and thus organizations should not rule out the alternative option of simply making a cash donation.

EPILOGUE

Our intention throughout this book has been to share our experience conducting research in the humanitarian sector over the past few years.

As mentioned in the beginning, this book only captures a portion of our experience and a few highlights of the main issues shaping the current state of humanitarian operations. In our interaction with our research partners we also acknowledge a need to further research areas like the following:

Erosion of Humanitarian Space: The increase in number of attacks on humanitarian workers over the past few years indicates the difficulties of accessing populations when humanitarian principles are compromised. These concerns lead us to reconsider the role of governments and the military in light of deteriorating security.

More Complex Disasters: Over the past few years we have seen an increase not only in disasters but also in their complexity, a worrisome trend in light of limited resources. This in addition to the fact that in a globalized society disasters have repercussions worldwide at least financially, if not politically.

Greater Demands and Needs for Transparency: Increased visibility provided by the media has led to better-informed donors who are demanding to know more about the impact of their donations. Information empowers individual donors to judge the efficiency of the aid organizations, making them compete for funding in the public eye. As a result, there is a decreased tolerance for bureaucratic systems that have failed in the past with duplication of efforts and delayed responses.

Professionalization of Humanitarian Logistics: Supply chain management has gained greater recognition in the humanitarian sector with organizations redesigning some of their departments to include best practices from the private sector. Subsequently, the need for training and education in logistics and supply chain management has risen, and modules and pedagogical materials need to be adapted. This is a particularly close area to our group given our investment over the past few years in case studies, a graduate-level elective, and an executive education program.

Changing Role of the Private Sector: The interaction between the private and the humanitarian sectors continues to be very dynamic with new models of engagement emerging after every big disaster. There is a need for better agreements on when and how companies can support humanitarian agencies, and better distinction between what could be considered pro bono and what is best done commercially. We also expect to see a more solid business case for humanitarian–private initiatives that create clear social (and economic) value.

Investment in Development Issues: Eventually there will need to be a greater focus from government, private, humanitarian, and development sectors on the root causes of most of the crises that plague us today such as climate change, energy consumption, territorial conflicts, access to healthcare, education, and poverty reduction; in short, the Millennium Development Goals.

In light of the challenges above, our book appears to be very timely. Better supply chain management will be a key ingredient in building a solid foundation for tackling the complex humanitarian problems of the future. We hope that this book inspires others to continue working in these areas, whether as academics, humanitarians, or representatives of the private sector.

We certainly are encouraged to continue our research and teaching in this field, as well as our many projects with humanitarian agencies and private corporations. If you are interested, do not hesitate to contact us.

4 December 2008
Rolando Tomasini, Humanitarian Research Group, Program Manager (Rolando.Tomasini@insead.edu).

Luk Van Wassenhove, INSEAD Social Innovation Centre, Academic Director and Henry Ford Chaired Professor of Manufacturing (Luk.Van-Wassenhove@insead.edu).

NOTES

1 Logistics of humanitarian aid

1. Van Wassenhove, Luk and Paul Kleindorfer. "Managing Risks in Global Supply Chains." *The INSEAD-Wharton Alliance on Globalizing: Strategies for Building Successful Global Business.* Wharton INSEAD Alliance, 2004.

2. Fine, Charles. *Clockspeed: Winning Industry Control in the Age of Temporary Advantage.* Perseus Book Group, 2001.

3. Handfield, Robert and Ernest Nichols. *Introduction to Supply Chain Management.* Prentice Hall, 1999.

4. Lee, Hau. "Triple-A Supply Chain." *Harvard Business Review.* October, 2004.

5. Ibid.

6. Handfield and Nichols. *Introduction to Supply Chain Management.*

7. Van Wassenhove and Kleindorfer. "Managing Risks in Global Supply Chains."

2 Humanitarianism

1. Ogata, Sadako. *Turbulent Decade.* W.W. Norton, 2005.

2. References to the Southern African food crisis of 2002 are inspired from Tomasini, Rolando and Luk Van Wassenhove. "Genetically Modified Food Donations and the Cost of Neutrality. Logistics

Response to the 2002 Southern African Food Crisis." INSEAD Case Study No. 03/2005-5169.

3. Keen, David. "The Economic Functions of Violence in Civil Wars." Adelphi Paper 320, London: International Institute for Strategic Studies (IISS), 1998.

4. Pictet, Jean. "The Fundamental Principles of the Red Cross." Geneva: Henry Dunant Institute, 1979.

5. Box inspired by the work of Stoddard, Abby. "Humanitarian NGOs Challenges and Trends." *Humanitarian Policies Group Report 14*. London: Overseas Development Institute, 2003. http://www.odi.org.uk/hpg/papers/hpgreport14.pdf

6. Minear, Larry. *The Humanitarian Enterprise: Dilemmas and Discoveries*. Kumarian Press, 2002.

7. MacFarlane, Neil. "Humanitarian Action: Conflict Connection." Occasional Paper #43. Thomas Watson Jr. Institute for International Studies, 2001.

8. Hoffman, Charles Antoine. "Measuring the Impact of Humanitarian Aid: A Review of Current Practices." *Humanitarian Policy Group Report 17*. Overseas Development Institute, 2004.

9. Ibid.

10. Ogata, Sadako. *Turbulent Decade*.

11. www.ifrc.org/news/av.asp

12. Minear, Larry. *The Humanitarian Enterprise: Dilemmas and Discoveries*.

3 Preparedness

1. Samii, Ramina and Luk Van Wassenhove. "IFRC Choreographer of Disaster Management – Hurricane Mitch." INSEAD Case Study No. 06/2002-5039.

2. Bohn, Roger. "Stop Fighting Fires." *Harvard Business Review*. July–August, 2000.

3. Handfield, Robert and Ernest Nichols. *Introduction to Supply Chain Management*. Prentice Hall, 1999.

4. Video from the IFRC website: http://www.ifrc.org

5. Samii, Ramina and Luk Van Wassenhove. "IFRC Choreographer of Disaster Management – Gujarat Earthquake." INSEAD Case Study No. 06/2002-5032.

6. Bohn, Roger. "Stop Fighting Fires."

4 Coordination

1. For more information on Civil–Military Coordination visit http://ochaonline.un.org/?TabId=1274

2. http://www.ochaonline.un.org

3. https://www.unjlc.org

4. UN Disaster Assessment Coordination (UNDAC) functions mainly in the initial period of natural disasters. Its primary role is to coordinate search and rescue operations.

5. UNJLC Training Material. Copenhagen 2004.

6. Abridged version of: Samii, Ramina and Luk Van Wassenhove. "UNJLC: The Afghanistan Crisis." INSEAD Case Study 02/2003-5092.

7. Based on personal interview provided in 2005 in Khartoum (Sudan).

8. Minear, Larry. *The Humanitarian Enterprise: Dilemmas and Discoveries.* Kumarian Press, 2002.

5 Information management

1. http://www.fundesuma.info/eng/about_us.htm. FUNDESUMA was created in 1996 as a non-profit, non-governmental organization, dedicated to the improvement of humanitarian supply management systems at the global level. It supports, promotes, and develops the SUMA methodology, assisting PAHO/WHO in technical and operational support, providing training in Latin America, the Caribbean, and globally, and maintaining and upgrading SUMA software.

2. www.paho.org. The Pan-American Health Organization (PAHO) is an international public health agency with 100 years of experience in working to improve health and living standards of the countries of the Americas. It serves as the specialized organization for health of the Inter-American System. It also serves as the Regional Office for the Americas of the World Health Organization and enjoys international recognition as part of the UN system.

3. Raynard, Peter. "Mapping Accountability in Humanitarian Assistance." ALNAP, 2002 [online]. http://www.alnap.org/pubspdfs/praccountability.pdf

4. Nicolas, Nestor and Richard Olson. "Independent-External Evaluation of SUMA and the 2001 El Salvador Earthquakes." Paper delivered to the PAHO, 2002.

5. http://www.fritzinstitute.org/PDFs/Case-Studies/Media_study _ExcSum.pdf

6. Tomasini, Rolando and Luk Van Wassenhove. "Managing Information in Humanitarian Crisis: The UNJLC Website." INSEAD Case Study No. 2005-5278.

6 Knowledge management

1. Tomasini, Rolando and Luk Van Wassenhove. "Managing Information in Humanitarian Crisis – The UNJLC Website." INSEAD Case Study No. 5218-2005.

2. Samii, Ramina and Luk Van Wassenhove. "The United Nations Joint Logistics Center (UNJLC) – The Afghanistan Crisis." INSEAD Case Study No. 5092-2003.

3. Handfield, Robert and Ernest Nichols. *Introduction to Supply Chain Management*. Prentice Hall, 1999.

4. *Humanitarian Supply Management and Logistics in the Health Sector*. Pan-American Health Organization, 2001.

5. Samii, Ramina and Luk Van Wassenhove. "Fuels: A Humanitarian Necessity in 2003 Post-Conflict Iraq." INSEAD Case Study No. 07/2005-5290.

6. Inspired by Galunic, Charles and John Weeks. "Managing Knowledge at Booz Allen & Hamilton: Knowledge On-Line and Off." INSEAD Case Study No. 08/2000-4846.

7 Building a successful partnership

1. Porter, Michael and Mark Kramer. "The Competitive Advantage of Corporate Philanthropy." *Harvard Business Review*, December, 2002.

2. Lee, Hau. "Triple-A Supply Chain." *Harvard Business Review*, October, 2004.

3. Tomasini, Rolando and Luk Van Wassenhove. "Overcoming the Barriers to a Successful Cross-Sector Partnership." The Conference Board Executive Action Report, 2006.

4. Tomasini, Rolando and Luk Van Wassenhove. "Fleet Forum: Rethinking Humanitarian Vehicle Management." INSEAD Case Study No. 5361-2006.

5. Tomasini, Rolando and Luk Van Wassenhove. "Moving the World: TNT–WFP Partnership – Looking for a Partner." INSEAD Case Study No. 2004-5187. Also see Samii, Ramina and Luk Van Wassenhove. "Moving the World: TNT–WFP Partnership – Learning to Dance." INSEAD Case Study No. 2004-5194.

6. Moss Kanter, Rosabeth. "From Real Change to Spare Change: The Social Sector as Beta Site for Business Innovation." *Harvard Business Review*, May, 1999.

7. Szulanski, Gabriel. *Sticky Knowledge: Barriers to Knowing in the Firm.* Sage Publications, 2003.

INDEX